Zen and the art of traveling

Heikki Nousiainen

The art of traveling

About movement and motion

Movement and motion have always been an important part of my life.

My other big passion, travelling is also movement, and searching. Writing is searching, a process, kind of movement. When I was writing this book, I found things that I did not expect to find.

Picasso claimed that he does not search, he finds. Maybe it is a creative, good way to deal with things in every aspect of life; not only in arts and literature.

Travelling can be a way to search your true self. Even tai chi (taiji) can be a journey inside, to research yourself.

I have been travelling all around the physical world both teaching tai chi and studying it. I am convinced that I had been travelling even without my passion to tai chi, but it has been an excellent way to learn to know new countries and people. As a tourist you are in a way always an outsider, and you can get only limited amount of information about how people live their lives and which values and thoughts guide their lives.

Tai chi is a taoistic martial art and Tao means a way or road. Tai chi is often compared with Chinas biggest river, even writing can be described as a river, meandering sometimes fast, sometimes slow. I found out under the working process of this book, how my passion for tai chi, writing and travelling are very closely interconnected. Their importance for me showed also to be greater than I had thought. During many years their importance has varied as in a good relationship; you should be able to change. Accept change and be able to be sometimes strong, sometimes weak, alternate instead having fixed roles. Unfortunately this is not often the case.

To write this book was great fun. The hardest thing was to limit the number of books and wise thoughts, that people have already written and said about travelling. I did not want to make this book a graveyard of citation. I take a solace of my plans to write more books, where I can tell things I had to exclude here. I find a graveyard of citation as a very good way to describe books and academic writings, where you do not trust on your own thinking, creativity and originality. I have also a tendency to hide me behind quotes of big thinkers. I was planning to use books that have a status as canon but decided to trust my own experiences and stories I have heard when travelling.

The social network you have at home is temporarily not there when you travel. In a way we are more vulnerable, unprotected and isolated from normal life when traveling, and I think it is a good thing.

You better keep your eyes and ears open, like a documentary film director Malik Bendellou did. He travelled around the whole world during one year, to find a good story. Finally he heard about a musician that had cult status in South Africa. He was told that the musician was dead but then he found out that he was maybe alive and kicking. He decided to find out what was true and he found the man, Sixto Rodriguez alive. Rodriguez had no idea that he was famous in South Africa, he had neither got any income for all the selling of his music that had been done there. He made a documentary film about it, "Sugar man", which has won a lot of prices in many countries.

There are interesting coincidences and connections with the director and me. Bendjellou was an actor when he was a child and I loved to go and see the films where he was acting. I hated Disney films and used to sleep in Disney productions, if it was possible for all the screaming that happens in them. I saw once a film with my youngest daughter where the director was acting, but I did not understand all the relations the adults had in the film. They had divorced and remarried cross and tick. I asked my daughter about the character the directors mother was playing and wondered who was her new husband in the film. My eight years old daughter started with words " Dad, it is obvious...". For my little daughter, the complicated network of relationships was totally clear, for me it was mysterious and complicated.

There is even one more personal connection between us. I contacted the director Bendjellou several times to get an interview with him. I wanted to travel to Sweden and do it but he did not have time. Finally he agreed and asked me to book a time for interview with his press secretary.

I never travelled to Sweden because Malik Bedjellou committed suicide a short time after our conversation in telephone. I was quite shocked about what had happened. I saw his picture in newspapers. In my mind was only a face of a boy who looked intelligent and friendly. Now I saw an adult man who did not have the strength to live after a long depression, although he could fulfill his dream and he achieved success, the most people do not even dare to dream of.

His journey is finished but his films continue to touch people. For example a Finnish man decide to find out who is the mystical Heikki, who Sugar man sings about. It showed to be a man from Estonia, who was active in labour union and a friend of Sixto. Many claim, that Sugar man is the real Bob Dylan. He has been living his own texts of his songs and not only inventing and lying about his background as Bob Dylan did. This being said, I am not denying Bob Dylan's talent. He was the first musician who got the Nobel Prize, so he is accepted everywhere.

Afterwards I have been thinking why I did not research about the man Heikki and continued my documentary, where the story of Sugar man was planned to be a part. I was maybe too shocked and quite often we do not see the things that happen near us, we think we have to search them far away from home. At home never happens anything. This is not true, everything happens near us and that is basicly what we can make art of. In books, films and paintings we have to know the things and proceedings, how could we describe something we have no knowledge of?

I had a favourite book for some time, I used to read some pages carefully in bed before falling asleep or I plocked it up from the bedside table when I could not sleep. The author of the book had sailed all the seven seas in a really little boat. His favorite idea was that if man wants to explain some phenomena in the physical world, man has to research and explain everything else in the world aswell. I think it is true but unfortunately it is a mission impossible. If you want to explain a phenomenon like tai chi, or traveling or why not writing, it starts to get complicated. Science can study only small areas at one time. There is evidence, that mankind once survived when arts and decoration started appear. We do not know if they have some causality, but it is very interesting. We can also have fantastic theories or guesses, even qualified such but we still cannot be sure. I know one thing and it is that I, as a writer and filmmaker, ask questions and study some aspects of reality. Politicians have the answers, or they say they have.

The idea to write about traveling came when I had discussions with a german Kali (martial art from

Philippine Islands) teacher. He told me that he hated traveling but loved to meet people in other countries and cultures, he even enjoyed to be there.

I did not have the heart to tell him, how releasing I had experienced the traveling to teach in different countries after a normal, busy week in my civil profession. At that time I had to work to be able to do my writing and teaching. I was working to finance my work that I considered my real work.

I also really enjoyed my flights from Asia back to Europe. The training there was hard in the very hot and humid climate, especially in Malaysia. I also felt the pressure, in a country, there is still death penalty in use and democratic and human rights are not necessarily applied. In many ways the country is modern and advanced but there are still sides I do not like. It was also so hot that after hard training I did not sleep much. It was absolutely fantastic to eat and drink and relax in a comfortable temperature in the plain and I felt safe.

I contemplated the opposite way to relate, for example what comes to poverty and violence. I have hard time to meet these things, when traveling, and all the good advices type (Learn to ignore it, you cannot help everybody) have not helped me.

Apparently some people are not finding these thing as troublesome. The german teacher was not worried about poverty and violence. In contrast, he envied the joy of life, the poor children showed every day amongst the poverty. He was wondering why he was not feeling himself happy in the middle of abundance of everything. He had the biggest BMW you could buy, the same with TV etc. I think he had made an observation that was important and I was thinking that he maybe learned more of traveling than me. We saw the same things but experienced and interpreted them differently.

The different ways to take a stand in front of problems and how to solve them are also interesting. If my studies in economics at the University level increased my caution and critical thinking, even leaning on known austerities, on different fields of knowledge, so studies in sociology was supporting my interest in different societies, cultures and ways of lives. I have accused University for decreasing creative thinking and spontaneous action. Even true entrepreneurship with too much analyzing and identifying problems and obstacles does not work. A true entrepreneur has to be somewhat crazy and invest all his/her time, money and effort, with other words risk everything. Both are good to have, theoretical knowledge and the right craziness to risk everything.

I had a Kung Fu teacher in Malaysia where socioeconomical conditions and power structures, even ethnicity influenced and dictated my training. We could not train in parks because gathering on public place was forbidden, even my teacher and me made a crowd, and people came to warn us that we can be arrested. This prohibition dated back to riots between chinese shop owners and malay people. Chinese people is a little minority but they control economical life.

My ambition with this little book is present different things that are connected with traveling, I outline different ways to travel. I am just thinking about a phenomenon called traveling.

Partly my interest is personal. Have I flied from or to something by traveling? Was it a solution to my problem, that I get bored very easily. I hope to get some answer during the writing process but I do not necessarily write about it, let see what happens.

What is fascinating us in traveling so tremendously? To see new places, experiences, meetings in different countries? Maybe motion? We are made to moving our bodies. We suffer now, and get sick of all sitting. Can it be change, coming home, to be able to tell about things to our families and loved ones, social prestige? I could continue the list, but instead I let my brain to continue the process. I am convinced that I will not get the final right answer, but hopefully I get new questions and learn a lot about different things. I hope this book is a report about some of my thoughts, and I can add a lot of new material after couple of years.

When I was working in a place, with Rudolf Steiners antroposofi as a guideline, I had a collaborator who was interested in traveling generally, and specifically in Greece. We worked with autistic children and had time in the evenings to exchange thoughts, because the children had to to bed quite early. Greece has been my favorite under decades, and because she knew places, which I did not know, so I listened to her stories with fascination. Autumn 2001 I got a very cheap flight and hotel in Greece quite late in the autumn. I told about this to my work-mate and hope she knew the place I was going to. The comment I received was " I would not like to go there this time of the year". I went to Greece, despite the expert was thinking, it was a bad idea. My time in Greece was one of the best I ever experienced when traveling. You can listen to opinions but be critical. I love to tell my students in martial arts about a definition of a good student. A good student listens very carefully what his/her teacher says, an excellent student thinks about what he/she heard and question it. I would like to add my own thing, a good student of Zen tries out the things on his/her own and evaluates if they work just for him/her. Just do it; like in the Nikes ad.

According to Mencius, the evil of a man is to be the teacher of others. This book tries to avoid it, although you can catch one or two advice or tip, if you read carefully.

My own theory about literature is that it can function as a consolation and inspiration. My late Kung Fu teacher, L. Leong (1999) used to say, that I should be happy if I get one of thousand people to change their life and be more healthy and happy by training. According to him, it is no use to think about the rest 999 persons as a failure. I hope that I manage to bring comfort and joy to some readers of this book. Enjoy.

The necessity of traveling

According to a latin proverb sailing is necessary, life is not. This saying reflects the values and reality of that time. Wealth was made by commerce and sailing enabled commerce. Nowadays to know Navigare necesse est, vivere non esset, is needed only to impress your company in an english pub. You can still see paintings with ships with that text under. Well, maybe even that era is finished already. As a young student I saw one in Plymouth.

I wanted to study languages but I was not interested to learn a dead language, latin. My fellow students, mostly female, knew the importance of latin, if you wanted to study on the University level. I wanted to learn to communicate. I was one of two who wanted learn french instead of latin of 183 students, so I did not get my chance.

When I teached in the monastery of Valamo, once a young munk drove me to airport. He was originally russian but talked perfect finnish. He told me that it was due to latin studies. He could understand the structure of a new language and it made it easy to learn whatever language. That impressed me but my goal is to communicate with people, to be able to follow the political life, cultural life, sports, be an active part of the society, so I still prefer living and changing languages.

Before I move on to describe my passion traveling, I want to make a program declaration. I do not believe that traveling is necessary. I fully understand people who do not like it, and even despise it. One of my good friends, psychologist, thinks that people like me who almost live for traveling or maybe even of traveling, are not the heroes. The real heroes are the people who go to their work every day, year after year and carry on. I can not disagree. The point is, that for me, traveling is necessary and I find it interesting, fascinating, broading my thinking and teaching me a lot of new things and giving new experiences.

This book is dedicated to people like me in the first place. Maybe some reflections interest even Brexit people, traveling has downsides and troubles, so why we continue doing it and do not simply stay at home?

About expectancies and preparations

What can be more enjoyable and generating more pleasure than, in the middle of a grey everyday life and its problems, dream just for a short moment about the future journey. Instantly we can move to a place, where we have booked a ticket, no matter if it is in a place with palm trees, in the alps, in a big city or on a little unknown island.

One very rainy Scandinavian summer was saved by a booked journey to Greece. I was having quite rough time in my private life and it helped me to get through that time by thinking about the future journey. I knew that after the summer I could relax in a nice warm place. It functioned as a mantra or the last straw, the main thing was that it helped me.

If you can afford it, I think that you can get addicted to travelling and waiting for next journey. For the most people their economic situation does not allow it, so it is better to enjoy the future journey with good conscious, when there is a possibility to do that. Maybe the pleasure of waiting for a journey has something to do with waiting for Christmas. For the most of us lucky ones, it brings back warm and pleasant memories. On the whole, child-mindedness and playing makes us creative and happy, it cannot be wrong to try to achieve that state of mind.

Before travelling I normally borrow books about the destination. I do not mean old basic tourist information but for example literature that takes place in that destination. I also buy a good map and basic guidebook, if I do not happen to have them already.

My Swiss friend showed me once all the maps he had bought during his many journeys. He had loads of them, maybe thousands. When I was cycling and walking through Europe I had to send maps back home at regular intervals. They took too much space and were unnecessary weight. When you are trekking it is good to have one map where you can see the whole picture, not only the more detailed maps. It was interesting to see where I was in the big picture, instead of only concentrating on the next day's stage. While waiting for the journey or trek you can study the maps in detail. I have a good tip on how to get a map to last even in rough conditions. Cover the map with plastic. The plastic should be glued on the map, so it will never break and you can draw your route on it. You can use it even when it is raining; it simply makes your trekking more pleasant. I learnt this when I took my pilot license. It was very practical to be able to plot important key points for aviation directly on the map, and draw your own course and then wipe it away before next flight.

Hit the road

Travelling and riding towards the sunset have lost a little bit of their magic. To say goodbye was more romantic and dramatic before the mobile phones era. Juhani Aho gives us a grasp on what it was like to take the road 100 years ago.

A young student is leaving to go to study at the University in the capital city and the whole family followes him to the harbour. There is also a girl who gave him mittens the day before. His friends are also there, even friends of the family. The young student is a little bit uncomfortable, but enjoys the people's interest at the same time. The bell rings and he has to go.

Mobile phones and internet allows us to be in contact all the time, so there is no need for dramatic goodbyes. There is no return without leaving, so I enjoy nowadays taking the road without too much sentimentality.

Trains are used in films as a symbol for leaving. Older Finnish audience will never forget when the actor Vesa- Matti Loiri was running after a train, which was transporting her mother away from him. The train is often used as a symbol for modern life, dangerous and threatening but at the same time fascinating and inexorable. The first film ever showed in public at the cinema was, precisely, a train arriving at the railway station.

The famous speechlessness of Scandinavians does not apply in trains, at least not on Friday nights in the restaurant car. The tradition of friendliness and the habit of small talk in trains is probably over soon and the situation becomes the same as on flights. The railway companies have already bought Italian trains with a design borrowed from McDonalds. Nobody wants to sit and chat in a plastic environment with colours which would be vulgar even in a child's room.

I am convinced that travelling in trains is going to be like aviation. We do not talk with people next to us, but we are sitting in our own bubble and we maybe communicate or we think that we communicate with the whole world. So far people tend to be more open in trains than in aeroplanes.

Maybe intriguing themes of leaving and coming back are one of the reasons which make even marginalized people to spend their time on railway stations. Naturally there are other reasons but who would not like to be alive and in touch with life, to go somewhere and to come back from somewhere.

One of my neighbours told me a true story about leaving. He had been sitting on a busstation drinking beer with people who did not go anywhere anymore. He was sickened, that nothing happened in his life anymore or in the group of people, he belonged to. One day he left the place and started to study in another city. After the studies he got a well paid job. He imagined that he could return to his old friends like in an American movie, everybody standing and applauding when he makes his entry. In a dream they also smiled admiring and supporting to him. In reality nobody saw him and he was totally rejected, when he decided to pay a visit one day, years later. He had become a threat to the group because he had proven that a change was possible.

The same neighbour became interested in my somewhat nomadic lifestyle or alternative lifestyle. How could you describe it, unusual, different? I warned him not to draw too hasty conclusions what my lifestyle means. I tried to get him understand that every choice has a meaning and consequences. You also pay a price, apart your choice but he did not want to listen. Above all this, he got many clients who were economically independent, retired aswell, but they did not know what to do with their lives after retirement. They had postponed the beginning of their lives after the next project and after the next etc. My neighbour did not want to be like these men, without friends, without hobbies, without interests. They only had money and time but nothing to do. The drinks on the beach with colourful umbrellas start to taste bad after some time if you are not already or becoming an alcoholic.

My neighbour told me that his salary was so good, that he could fulfill all his desires, even travelling to exotic places but he resigned and started sailing around the world, completely without experience about sailing. He told me that he would get work, if he managed to come back. Maybe only telling about his experiences would be enough to keep him alive. I never heard anything about him after that. I hope he got warm and friendly winds on his journey.

It is not necessary to make such drastic breakaways. I think about Chinese saying that if you are made for flying you should fly, some of us are different and have to fly because it is their nature. I do not think that it is a question of extreme poles and of a choice between them; An office job from eight to five or nomadic life style for years or decades. Nowadays it is exciting enough whether you can get a job and eventually keep it.

All the choices have consequences. I taught tai chi in France in a beautiful area of Loire River with castles reminding me more of a fairy tale than real castles. A German participant told me how he had before worked in Germany at summer time, and then he had spent the winters in Asia. He travelled around and made gewgaw. When he came back to Germany, after the winter, he brought with him a container of clothes, worked the whole summer in hospital again, long hours, went to Asia and...

He was now tired of his lifestyle but could not stop it because working eight to five did not interest him. The problem was also that he was about to be without money when retired, because he had been working so little in Germany.

I think that the most important thing is that we create our life so that we are happy with it. It is not easily done, most of us are not really working with things that we do want to work with. For me it took a lifetime to be able to do the things I really want to do, but I am happy I reached my goal, even though late in life.

I met a man in my work when I was twenty. He was eighty and was living in a care home. I was thinking about earning money but he told me that a real human being has to protest against something every day. At least it kept him young. Care home is normally considered more like a waiting room for the final journey than a place you make a voyage. I experienced many voyages there, among these old people. I travelled with them far away to other places, other countries; other times. The journey went often to my own country that did not exist anymore, because the times they had been changing. The old people could tell me about the tools and working methods that I had never heard about, because new tools and methods had replaced the old. Anyway, they had the energy and desire to tell me about these things and I had time and energy to listen, especially because during that time I did not have to clean or cook .....

Shortly about Zen and Tao

Three books that deal with traveling have been important for me during a longer time in my life. Two of them deals also with Zen. Zen is in chinese Chan, which is an important concept in many martial arts which I have been practicing and teaching over thirty years. I have practiced Japanese arts, for example four different karate styles, although my speciality are the Chinese arts. Later years I have been interested in Indonesian martial arts and arts from Philippine Islands.

There are many similarities between for example Chinese and Japanese arts and their philosophies.

Karate even means Chinese hand or the art of Chinese hand. First during the second World War Karate was made a tool for the Japans army and in Japan Karate became empty hand, originally important weapons traing was excluded. In Okinawa you can visit a karatemuseum and there are karate weapons. Techniques with and without weapons were described as a relationship between sister and brother. Old Okinawa masters bowed in the direction of China. There is no empty hand mentioned anywhere. Old Okinawa karatemasters liked to tell stories, where they had been travelled and trained in China for years. Historians have detected that some weeks stay could change to months and years in the stories. It has taken a lot of effort to come at least somewhat near the truth. Some stories are still in the mystical darkness of ancient times and maybe it is better that they can remain that way. A certain amount of exotic and esoteric aura is totally ok, even though I have taken it as my mission to open up the curtain of secrecy and mysticism. Most of the time, under the sometimes heavy curtains, are totally logical things. They though take time and effort to master. They are hard enough to understand and master, so there is no need to complicate these fantastic things, which the old masters, ancient geniuses invented and developed.

Eugen Herrigel describes his study of Zen in the book Zen and the art of archery. He was staying several years in Japan and besides his work at the University, teaching philosopy, he studied Kyudo, the art of archery.

The first two years he had to study without the bow and arrow.

His little book is a masterpiece and it is suitable to read in small doses. I like the clarity of writing when he describes things that actually are very hard to comprehend.

One of the big themes in the book is waiting and it is a topic interests me even on the personal level. Words are not enough to characterize and understand Zen and Tao. The canon of Taoism, Tao te ching, begins with words " The Tao you can talk about is not the real Tao". This is a logical somersault, everything after that sentence becomes false. Zen uses often so called koans. They are not logical, instead they try to provoke the mind. I can make an example here, " Was the book of Zen and the art of travelling treating the theme with respect before the book was written?".

I used this little book whe I tested my students for the black belt. I stressed physical training in my tuition and that is why the young people were so surprised when they should read this little book before the black belt test. They did not have to like it but they should have an opinion and show that they have read it. Nobody liked it, the most usual feedback was, why should they read it?

I hoped that the book would function as an easy introduction to more difficult writings and maybe reading in general. There is a theory about intoxicants that mild ones are an introduction to more heavy and dangerous one, from beer to heroin. I hoped to get the same effect what comes to reading. I do not know how it went, but the people I teached have been successful in their lives. It is another thing if they got a goodlife, which can be also a goal in Asian martial and health arts. They go together, martial and health/good life. Asian martialarts can be seen, as one way, to achive a happy, even wise way of life.

Under the working process of this book I found out, that Herrigel had been a real hard-core nazi. I was as surprised about this fact as I found out, that Knut Hamsun, the writer of many excellent books - only to mention " Hunger " had been nazi in Norway.

This is actually an ancient problem. Is it the art we should focuse on, the beayty of the artist;s work or should we pay attention on his/her opinions and actions. Does a masterpiece lose it's value, if the master has been doing unmoral things, or even worse.

I do not know if I had been interested to read these gentlemen if I had known their background.

Maybe I was lucky not having the knowledge?

Robert M. Pirsig was trying to publish his book a long time. Every publisher in USA said no.

Finally one publisher who was already planning his retirement, decided to make an act of cultural charity. He did not believe he could sell any of Pirsig's books, but the contrary happened.

The book Zen and the art of motorcycle maintanance was a big success in many countries and it has been used in University courses as a textbook. Everybody knows the saga how Harry Potters writer was treated by the publisher. In Pirsig`s case I can understand the publishers, because the book is not easy to read, especially without, at least basic, University studies. On one level travelling happens with a motorcycle but there is also a journey to history, philosophy, the meta theory of science, even madness. Physically travelling happens along small roads in the USA, but the real topic is the differences how you can reason about the world and how man reason in East and West. It makes the reading more interesting and rewarding if you know the basic scientific reasoning.

The main person in the book is travelling with his son and two friends with motorcycles. The couple they travel with, do not like technology. If their motorcycle has any troubles they phone a mechanic right away and leave their motorcycle for maintanance. The main character is relating to his motorcycle and its maintenance in a Zen way. He cares about the maintenance and serves his motorcycle almost ritualistically with great accuracy and time. I did not have a motorcycle when I read the book for the first time. I own one now and I have to admit that I belong in the groupn, not interested in technology.

The message of the book could be crystallized so that the maintenance of a motorcycle is purest Zen if your attitude is caring, and you do it with maximal concentration and accuracy. This fascinates me, because this kind of thinking converts even crocheting to meditation, especially it is so, if the person doing it perceives it in such a way. Thanks to this book I am no longer so hostile related to all technology, like before. I have even started to do some maintenance myself with help of another techonology, internet. With help of internet, I found information and help how do the basic maintenance on your own motorcycle. Very good and easy to follow instructions. I am hopeless in the real world, concerning fixing things. I am comfortable in the world of books. If internet can make a hopeless bookperson to a motorcycle mechanic, so maybe I can learn more about the world of computers in the future?

With the help of books I made my first journeys. I still feel the tickling sensation of thrill when I read the first sentence in Juhani Aho's book, written more than 100 years ago. " In the harbour of Kuopio the bells of the departing boats rang the second time".

In the same way flings Robert M. Pirsig us somewhere on the motorcycle, where, that we do not know, yet. " Without removing my left hand from the motorcycle I can see my watch and that it is eight thirty am. Even though the speed is 95 km an hour, the wind is warm and humid ".

Apart if you are a biker or not, you can sense his words, feel the warm wind on your face and experience the thrilling feeling of freedom in your chest.

A finnish author and journalist, Juhani Aho maybe have a strange record. He was nominated for the Nobel price in literature twelve times! I will deal with Juhani Aho's book -To Helsinki- further on but can mention already that I became surprised aswell as interested in his radicalism and the modern touch in his books. The themes themselves have been written and told in arts uncountable times but never just the way he does it. I have found this quality mos often in french literature. He has a French quality in his writing, by this I mean the ability to find a totally new angle how to describe a dramatic story. He describes the language debate that was going that time. Swedish speaking did not consider Finnish as a enough advanced language for the University level. The funny thing in this context is, that it was precisely the opinion in Europe, about Swedish language, but everything went well in both countries. English has today conquered both Scandinavian languages in the Universities and soon in all bigger companies.

Longing for somewhere else

Tove Jansson created the Moon family. The father of that imaginary family is a jovial type, he loves to sit on the veranda, sipping whiskey and smoking a pipe. The paradise like state of affairs begins to sneak by anxiety and anguish. Moon pappa is belonging to somewhere else, far away from home. Moon mother understands her man's belonging and somehow accepts it. This acceptance of the other persons needs and desires makes the story fantastic. She is convinced that she will get her husband back, if she can tolerate his need and desire. That is in fact what happens in the story, she gets her husband back and more satisfied with life on the veranda.

We all get tired and blasé sometimes. Our society and culture can be oppressing too. If not before so when you get children, can life seem to be like a prison. Sometimes our life situation is pressing. To break with grey everyday does not need a journey to Bahamas. Change apartment with a friend who is living in the countryside or vice versa if you live in rural areas. A night at a hotel, in the same city you live in, is also a possibility.

Tai chi or some other activity can take you on a life long and exciting journey. In a film of Italian director Moretti, psychotherapist gets sicken of a chattering patient. He goes to a cabinet, opens the doors. The cabinet is full of running shoes and the therapeutist tells the patient that this is his solution for boredom and anguish. Maybe not according the handbook of a therapeutist but very impressive.

Modern parents bestow each other possibility to travel on their own and many grandparents are nowadays in so good condition, that they are happy to take care of grandchildren, when the parents are traveling. I have preferred to take children with me if possible. The only negative thing is that children get this hunger for world and learn to demand more of life. I have had the best time when traveling with my children, of course it has to happen quite much on the conditions of the children. Your own needs and desires you can fulfill some other time.

I was in Cyprus with my youngest daughter and made a big mistake by ordering meze. The waiter was very friendly and he explained enthusiastically how he spent almost seven hours with his friends eating this much meze. For us it took twenty minutes and then my daughter wanted to go and we left. She was too little to enjoy restaurant visit, nowadays it is the best thing she knows. Homecoming is also easy with children, you do not have time to experience emptiness and melancholy.

I was so interested to go on a voyage, before that I did to want t come back. I was belonging somewhere else already when coming back home from a journey. This has changed over the time. To return and stay at the same place is as interesting as traveling. I am comfortable everywhere. It started actually after a period of quite severe turmoil in my life. I got divorced and noticed, that if I was traveling I reached some kind of vacuum, where I was not feeling sad. Little by little I started to feel happy everywhere.

I do no longer have the urgent need to travel but I like it. During the process of writing this book I have experienced many of my journeys again, even the feelings and emotions which were connected to those wanderings. When my memory has failed I have been able to check the places I have visited on the internet. I could not recall a name of a little restaurant in Milan. Virtually I could return there, because I recalled the way there from the place I had the accommodation. So I followed the path and stopped in front of the restaurant and checked the name, by focusing at the name, quite amazing for a person being born in fifties.

I perhaps lied a little bit, to hit the road is still more important than to come back, besides without going away there is no coming back.

Traveling as a solution to our problems

We can run away from our selves and our problems.
I had to witness a middle-aged couples marriage
crisis on the island of Crete. It was not voluntarily,
me and my friend had a room next to the couple.
They fought without a stop, but when they landed
to the dining room, they had both sunglases and
they were very lovely. They were polite to each
other and started always with words like " Darling,
could you hand me the salt, please". They continued
immediately the row, after they went back to their

hotelroom. I could only try to guess what made they quarrel so mercilessly. At least they did not wash their dirty laundry in public.

We do not spend so much time together in normal life but when traveling we are together all the time. You have to be able to communicate with each other and have a good relationship in order to manage to have a nice vacation. There is no place to unify a relationship, I think.

Crete had not so many tourists at that time and it was a special voyage, because it was my first journey to a foreign country I paid myself. I had been working in a brewery the summer months I was free from school. I wonder today, why we had booked so fine hotel with three course's dinner included in the price. We did not spend any time at the hotel, so the cheapest hostel had been ok. Our own marital problems were still in the future, but we did get some foretaste what marriage can be. This was the first and last time I spent whole days at the beach. Vi were sunbathing on the beach, although it was actually too hot to lie in the sun. We did not feel good, but we were determined to use our time well, so we enjoyed sun and beach for every penny we had paid. The colour in our face disappeared after a week in chilly Scandinavian. I made a decision, that for me an half an hour or one hour is enough on the beach in one day, and it has functioned well. I enjoy to go to beach everyday, especially after running or training something else first. I have no desire to suffer on the beach. After a swim it is wonderful to let the sun dry you and warm the whole body, especially nice if you have aching muscles. It is like massage, very relaxing, after that you are ready for a new day and all its problems. I have not been able to avoid quarrels but I also decided; because of the couple we had to listen, that I do not want use the time I am traveling to dispute with someone, that decision I have managed to keep. I became very happy when my daughter told me on Malta, winter 2004 that we get along much better, than she does with her friends when traveling.

The song of homesickness (Roadmovie) is maybe not familiar everywhere but it is a kind of road movie where father and son try to find understanding for each other during a journey to the place they spent most of their lives. Father and son did find some basic unity and understanding and the healingprocess could begin.

Sometimes the worst sides of us can appear during a journey. I asked once my friend, who was planning to ski for months in the mountains, if I could make him company one week. He told me that if I could keep my mouth shut so then it would be green light. According to him people who hire a wilderness guide become very strange and cannot do anything on their own but are willing to critize and give advice to the guide. I promised to be quiet and I got an unforgettable experience in the Sarek national park, northern part of Sweden, near the boarder of Norway. The mobile phones did not function during that week and we met only a couple of people but the views were fantastic. It is not only a fun place, if you do not have respect for the nature. Every year they find tourists dead, who have not been able to count their strength and endurance right. Many has still food and something warm to drink in the backpack, they have only stopped for a rest. The interesting thing is that most have opened their jacket, because body is gathering the warmth near vital organs; like the heart. Their last sensation was a warm feeling in the breast. These kinds of incidents are hard to stop and to be honest, we had one day where we had calculated our daytrip wrong and we were exhausted when we reached our goal just before the darkness fell. When you are trekking and the terrain is hard you have to use concentration that reminds you of Zen. You are only and fully concentrated on the next step or the next movement with your skies. You cannot reach the mountain top without a certain kind of animal skin or leather that makes your skiing more walking than skiing. On the top of the mountains, there are no trees protecting you from the cold wind and it consumes your energy much quicker than you can think of. At the same time when I was in the mountain and skiing during demanding weather conditions, I was thinking about my life which had stagnated and was focused too much on accomplishing things, instead of creating and really living my life. I had to have three mobile phones on me because of the work; I was not happy with my situation although I was making decent money. The nature was formidable and my problems seemed very undistinguished and as I already mentioned my phones did not function so I had no immediately preceding problems to solve.

When we got exhausted, we stopped and took more clothes on us from the backpack. We could not sit but we were standing and drinking warm coffee and eating dried food that the army is using also.

After a stop you got more courage and strength and you could carry on, especially your mind was more hopeful and your selfconfidence gets better after the body gets some fuel. Even though you are pendling somewhere near your limit, what you really are able to do physically, it is easy compared to the hundreds of challenges everyday life means today. The mechanic movement becomes like meditation or hypnosis. Afterwards you sleep well because you are naturally tired and you have got plenty of fresh air aswell. It would be to make things too uncomplicated to claim that I found the right answers to my problems during that trekking. The only thing I know is that a process started in the mountains and after about a year or two I made some radical changes in my life, hopefully to the better direction, that is what I believe

About expectancies and preparations

What can be more enjoyable and generating more pleasure than, in the middle of a grey everyday life and it's problems, dream just for a short moment about the future journey. Instantly we can move to a place, where we have booked a ticket, no matter if it is in a place with palm trees, in the Alps, in a big city or on a little unknown island.

One very rainy Scandinavian summer was saved by, an early in the spring booked journey to Greece I had haft quite rough time in my private life and it helped me to get through that time by thinking about the future journey. I knew that after the summer I could relax in a nice, warm place. It functioned as a mantra or the last straw, the main thing is that it helped me.

I think that you can get addicted to travelling and waiting to travell, if you can afford it. For the most people their economic situation does not allow it, so it is better to enjoy the future journey with good conscious, when there is a possibility to do that. Maybe the pleasure of waiting for a journey has something to do with the waiting for the Christmas. For the most of us lucky ones it brings back warm and pleasant memories. On the whole, child-mindedness and playing makes us creative and happy, it can not be wrong to try to achieve that state of mind.

Under the time before a journey I normally borrow books about the destination. I do not mean old basic tourist information but for example literature that take place in the destination. I buy also a good map and basic guidebook, if I do not happen to have them already.

My Swiss friend showed me once all the maps he had bought during his many journeys. He had loads of them, maybe thousands. When I was cycling and walking through Europe I had to send maps back home at regular intervals. They took too much space and were unnecessary weight. When you are trekking it is good to have one map where you can see the whole picture, not only the more precise maps. It was interesting to see where I was in the big picture, instead only concentrate on the next days stage. While waiting for the journey or trek you can study the maps leisurely. I have a good tip for how to get a map last even rough conditions. The map you need to use often is good to cover with plastic. The plastic should be glued on the map so it will never break and you can draw on it your route. You can use it even when it is raining, it simply makes your trekking more pleasant. I learned this when I took a pilot license. It was very practical to be able to plot important limits for aviation direct on the map and draw your own course and then wipe it away before next flight.

All these activities are more enjoyable foretaste of the future journey, I do not make detailed planning, actually I support the idea of spontanious and free travelling. This is depending of course of what kind of journey I am planning. When I was hiking along Via Francigena I was following the old pigrimige route but the longer I hiked the more liberties I took. I heard an interview with a woman who also make long hikes. She shared my experience that in the beginning it is a question of honour to walk or cycle to the bitter end. Later she learned to take it easy and for example take a train one day of the body needed rest and it did not mean giving up anything. Before it had been like a sacrilege or defeat. It is good to have alternative plans for hiking in mind. Some people plan a one months trelleborg in detail. They plan how many kilometers they walk every day and book accomodation for the whole month. In this way you spare a lot of money and time, plus stress and you are safe but you have another stress. Everyday you have to do your kilometers even if your body is hurting and you need a day to rest and maybe wash your clothes and take a look at something interesting, so you cannot do that. You have to carry on. Naturally if you do not book in advantage you have to search for accomodation when you are tire and risk not to get any place or to get an very expensive accomodation. On the other side you have your freedom. I prefer this way. If I find an interesting place I stay maybe one more night and visit interesting places, take photos, eat good and relax. If you are on a long teen anything can happen. Problems with knees, back and muscles are very usual. Of course you can also have some kind of minor accident.

You should be well prepared physically if you plan a long trek. You have to train months before you start and if you buy special shoes you have to start to keep them longer and longer times at home. You are asking for troubles if you start trekking with new shoes. Normally people use too heavy shoes. The terrain dictates what kind of shoes you should have. I used many years too heavy shoes only because I felt more professional with robust, heavy shoes. If the terrain is quite easy use light shoes. Only in a demanding terrain with rocks and very uneven terrain you need really expensive and robust shoes. The special shoes need use so think twice before you buy them. This being said, it does not mean that you have to save money when buying shoes. No, you have to buy the shoes you need. There are a lot of books about this topic but basicly you need good shoes, good backpack and two t-shirts, two pairs of good socks and underware, preferably marino wool. It warms even when wet and it does not smell sweat.

around and made gewgaw. When he came back to Germany, after the winter, he brought with him a container of clothes, worked the whole summer in hospital again, long hours, went to Asia and...

He was now tired of his lifestyle but could not stop it because eight to five work did not interest him. The problem was that he was about to be without money when retired because he had been working so little in Germany.

Longing for somewhere else

The father Tove Jansson created, in his world famous books about Moomin family, is a jovial type, he loves to sit on a veranda, sipping whiskey and smoking a pipe. The paradise like state of affairs begins to sneak by anxiety and anguish. Moomin pappa is belonging to somewhere else, far away from home. Moomin mother understands her man's belonging and accepts it. This This acceptance of the other persons needs and desires makes the story fantastic. She is convinced that she will get her husband back if she can tolerate his need and desire. That is in fact what happens in the story, she gets her husband back and more satisfied with life on the veranda.

We all get tired and blasé sometimes.Our society and culture can be oppressing too. If not before so when you get children, can life seem to be like a prison. Sometimes our life situation is pressing. To break with grey everyday does not need a journey to Bahamas. Change apartment with a friend who is living on the countryside or vice versa if you live on a country side. A night at a hotel in the same city you live in is also a possibility.

Tai chi or some other activity can take you on a life long and exciting journey. In a film of Italian director Moretti, psychotherapist gets sicken of a chattering patient. He goes to a cabinet, opens the doors. The cabinet is full of running shoes and the therapeutist tells the patient that this is his solution for boredom and anguish. Maybe not according the handbook of a therapheutist but very impressive.

Modern parents bestow each other possibility to travel on their own and many grandparents are nowadays in so good condition, that they are happy to take care of grandchildren, when the parents are traveling. I have preferred to take children with me if possible. The only negative thing is that children get this hunger for world and learn to demand more of life. I have had the best time when traveling with my children, of course it has to happen quite much on the conditions of the children. Your own needs and desires you can fulfill some other time.

I was in Cyprus with my youngest daughter and made a big mistake by ordering meze. The waiter was a friendly man and he explained enthusiastically how he spent almost seven hours with his friends eating this much meze. For us it took twenty minutes and then my daughter wanted to go and we left. She was too little to enjoy restaurant visit, nowadays it is the best thing she knows. Homecoming is also easy with children, you do not have time to experience emptiness and melancholy.

I was so interested to go on a voyage before that I did to want t come back. I was belonging somewhere else already when coming back home from a journey. This has changed over the time. To return and stay at the same place is as interesting as traveling. I am comfortable everywhere. It started actually after a very heavy period in my life. I got divorced and noticed that when I was traveling I reached some kind of vacuum, where I was not feeling sad. Little by little I started to feel happy everywhere.

I do no longer have the urgent need to travel but I like it. During the process of writing this book I have experienced many of my journeys again, even the feelings and emotions which were connected to those wanderings. When my memory has failed I have been able to check the places I have visited on the internet. I could not recall a name of a little restaurant in Milan. Virtually I could return there, because I recalled the way there from the place I had the accommodation. So I followed the path and stopped in front of the restaurant and checked the name, by focusing at the name, quite amazing for a person being born in fifties.

I perhaps lied a little bit, to hit the road is still more important than to come back, beside without going away there is no returning back home.

Change

What if we are in so happy position that traveling has started to feel routine and less interesting. This may sound as a luxury problem for many of us, but the fact is that more and more people can travel a lot, and they do.

You can change your habits and preferences.

If you have before always traveled alone, try to travel with friends or a group of people you do not know. One of the most intressenting experiences I have had, was when I and my friend decided to travel to Italy with persons we did not actually know at all. Only one person in the little group knew us all, and we had been his friends for years, so we did not feel unsafe in any way. Except that during traveling everything can happen, and we did not know, if we could get along with each other;

We met once before the journey, where we made up the rules, if you can call them so. Actually it was more an agreement that there are no rules, no musts to do or behave in a certain way, and absolutely no must to be together all the time. We agreed, that all of us had the right to do things on their own or do nothing without the disapproval of the rest of the group. We decided that we usually would try to eat dinner together, to be able to share our experiences, but even that was not obligatory.

In reality, we were quite much together, all the time, but it never felt as a must, what we call a forced bun. Some mornings we met on the beach before sunset and trained together qi gong, when the sun went up. It is worth the early awakening. One morning we took the motorcycles and drove to the mountains in the dark. We climbed up to the mountain top, which we had checked in the daylight so that it was safe to climb. Climbing in this case was not advanced climbing with ropes, but enough to give us a serious morning exercise . On the mountain top my friend guided us in a meditation session and with my guidance we did tai chi and qi gong. The place was magnificent, mountains on one side and the blue sea on the other side. I was so inspired of the place, that I made an exception and had a demonstration for my friends, in tai chi spear/staff. Normally I do not like to demonstrate, it is not part of the art in my mind.

Finally we climbed down to the valley and drove in a small village for brunch. We went to a place where the owner had to go buy something for our breakfast and he put a bottle of Ouzo for us to spend the time with, during his absence.My friends used the opportunity and you can imagine that it had an effect on an empty stomach after exercising several hours and it was still morning. I was hungry and started to be irritated. My friends did not understand my irritation and that was one of the few moments we almost started to fight, but managed to avoid it. After eating, we were more than pleased with our excursion and the world was smiling even at me. It had been a better idea to order breakfast with us and we could have eaten it at the mountain top with a view, but maybe next time we are wiser. We were all very pleased to travel together and I can recommend it but, with a top tip, everything can happen. Every group have their own dynamics. I have teached groups which were harmonious with good humour and a humanistic way of reasoning. We were growing together. Sometimes the opposite has happened, like in a relationship. When things go bad people can figuratively, even literally, destroy each other.

Blood sugar levels were involved every time things got a little tensed in our group. I have learned how drastic it can be from my daughter. Her mood changes much more rapidly than mine, but it is easy to control by letting her eat regularly. I hope every problem in life could be so easily fixed.

My ex-xife's dad traveled to the same place during decades in the winter time. I have never tried that but I can understand the advantages. You do not have to use time and energy to explore all the new places (It is great fun). Even the people can be familiar(normally the staff changes every year) and you can get better service and, if you are lucky, you get new friends. My father-in-law loved the sun and he used all his time on the beach and the evenings with good food and wine. He was 93 when he took his children and grandchildren with him the last time to the sun. There was one son with family missing but he said that next year is going to be their turn. That did not happen anymore, but his spirit was high to the end and I admire him for that.

You can find sun worshippers at strange places. I was teaching tai chi at Valamos monastery during many years. I was told that one of the monks who loves the sun, has a permission to travel to Gran Canaria every winter and sunbathe a week! Valamos monastery in Eastern Finland is definitively a place to recommend. I was always happy to go there and I was happy to leave. I went home quite much heavier because the food is so good and despite training all the days I put on some weight every time I visited the orthodox monastery.

Arto Paasilinna has been translated to english and fifty other languages. In one of his books an old commercial counselor do not want to travel anymore, because in his case it means that he drinks brandy on the balcony the whole week. Maybe it should be time to try to be sober and do things? If you only lie on the beach on vacation, try to learn something new. Many of us continue to perform even during the vacation. Maybe drinking brandy and lie on the beach would be the ideal relaxation for that type of people.

I saw an interesting documentary of a family holiday in the sun. The father of the family arranged all kinds of activities for his two children and wife. They visited waterparadise, they sat on a huge banana behind a fast boat. He hired a jeep and they drove around the countryside and visited nearby cities. All the days were full of activities.

When the family was once again heading to new adventures in a boat, the director of the documentary asked the kids, what was the best with the whole vacation. The answer was; to be able to be together with mam and dad.

I can recognice the anxiety of the father. I had the same problem in the beginning of the vacation in our country cottage. I even started building projects and I am actually not suited for practical things.

After couple of weeks the mind and body calmed down and to feed sheep together with my children or to go after drinking in the harbour was enough with activities for a whole day.

I have never liked changes and maybe it is the reason why I train tai chi, where the change is the most important thing. I practise also to change everything in my life every now and then. This is important for us old school boys, who maybe did not live our lives as we wished, but followed the family tradition and the rules and expectations of the society. When I started to practise tai chi, I also decided not to hurry, only diligently practise and not worry too much. I wanted to be good in twenty years and now, even that number is doubled, I still learn new things. Actually I learn faster now than ever, eventhough the physical level of my aging body can not be the same anymore. There are ways to compensate even that.

Sometimes the change means that certain doors get closed. Happily you are always welcome to the world of books and arts. The only thing I wanted to own was books. I had collected quite a number of books, when one of my longer journeys forced me to get rid of them. It was sad. I even sold my sportscar and my flat but they were not important. Some time before my journey I started to read the books I red as a teenager or young adult. It was an experience to see that quite many books still were impressive and some I liked even more than before. Naturally some had lost their magic power but it was very few.

One of the books I had to give away, was Roland Barths book, the floating opera. He wrote it as a young man and there the main character has the idea that you should break all your habits but keep one untouched, to prevent not to loose yourself.

Change and movement was the main themes in the book. There was also the idea that the operaboat should move slowly along the river and people would see only some part of the play.

Most of the expeditions to the exciting world of literature I made in a cellar of a bookshop, where world literature was sold for about one dollar/pound/euro, as a pocket book, mostly. I could buy several classics every time I visited the bookshop and travel round the world, even as a poor student who hardly had enough money for food. Nowadays I wonder, how could we afford to drink so muh beer?

English chocolate cake

I was in Brixham, England 1975 one month, staying in a family and studying english in a school daytime.

Englishmen had an other idea about the course. They called it sex and beer course. We did not get upset about that, I think we were pleased, but in reality it was quite innocent time.

I did not eat chocolate at all, that time and I especially hated cakes. I did not realize that englismen can bake cakes that tastes heavenly good, small miracles. I tasted one. I was hooked. I did not know about Proust`s Madeleine cookie at that time and if I did, it did not matter to me. I have since then tried to find the same taste everywhere and I am still searching. I have tried to describe the taste to professional people in different ways, the simplest is that it is near Brownie, or at least it is the right direction. I think it was a family recipe and maybe not possible to get anywhere, one of it`s kind.

I experience foreign countries till a certain degree by scents, even smells, flavors and how food and drink taste. A young person has not so many experiences and all the senses are more open. I miss the magical sense of feeling of different places I had as a child and young adult. I cannot sense it as strong anymore. Maybe it was chi/ki, lifeforce, that could give those sensations? I suppose everybody can recognize that in their own lives?

Anyway I learned an important lesson in England. Try everything without prejudices. It includes really everything, not only food. I still like England and eglishmen, especially the politeness, manners and how they are willing to help even tourists. Food is maybe not the first thing you associate with the country, allthough in London you can get the best food of every country you can think of. Fish and chips is still on my list when I visit England, but once is enough.

I often think what foreigners think about our way to cook crabs still living and then the final countdown, mämmi, the food we eat at Easter. I have never liked it and I understand people who do not want to taste it. Another Scandinavien strange food, from Sweden, is the fish that smells really bad. I think it is a delicacy, allthough when I was served it the first time, I thought it was a practical joke. One more peculiar dish, for most visiters is the sausage/potato mix you buy after a long night in bars. Mixed with loads of mustard and ketchup it is not something you normally eat, but tastes fantastic after enough with beer.

Every country has similiar things and I love to explore. I do not feel the pressure to like everything but I want to try everything.

To try new things does not mean hunting of new experiences. Everybody do not need to jump down from a mountain top without parachute, so called sky diving. I do not think extreme things have anything to do with the interest of new people, new phenomen or new things. It does not mean the opposite either.

Let`s go back to Englan in seventiees. As a young person I found a strange inconsistency in the attitudes, behavior and reasoning of the father in the house. He was often time talking badly about immigrants, but his workmate and friend in the pubevenings was a black man. I was not a diplomat at that point and I asked how his talking and walking was connected. He was very surprised and said that Henry is his friend, it is different!

I did not get it then. I understand it now. If you learn to know somebody, you talk with a human being, not with an abstract concept like immigrants. I am a little bit ashamed of myself, that I confronted the poor man so directly. At the same time, I like the honest desire to understand the world and challenge the things that seemed to be wrong.

I have nowadays one of my most important martial arts teachers in south of England. I have often thaught that maybe I should visit the little coastal city, Brixham and try to locate the house. Would it be wise? The family had small children when I stayed with them and were not so much older than me, so there is a big chance that they both still live in the house. Is it better to keep my dear memory as it is; dear? But what if the couple were there and a chocolate cake was waiting on the kitchen table and I could finally get the chance to taste it again?

Remote longing

The need to sometimes escape everyday life is not a modern phenomenon. I had this fallacy until I trekked over 2000 kilometers from Canterbury, England to Rome along an old pilgrimage route, Via Franzigena. I walked and cycled with a bicycle without gears. There are plenty of evidence, even texts, that wittness that people had the same remote longing then, and they did travel, espeially when the spring came.

My old school had placed so high, that a young man could not dream and watch out. I saw only the sky and it nourished my imagination, which was quite lively. I was feeling like sitting in a prison and I wanted to get out and be free. Especially the spring time was hard, almost unbearable. One of my favorite fantasy was to drive my car (I did not have one) until I came enough south to experience warm spring and then finally to mediterrian sea and summer. I was lucky that I did not know that I had to wait almost forty years to fulfill my dream. 2013 I drove south and on the Swiss side it was snowing heavily but after passing St Gotthard tunnel, I came out on the Italian side and there was summer. I stopped my car and me and my friend went out and enjoyed the sun and the warm weather. It was incredible. We were feeling warm, only having shorts and t-shirt and it was snowing on the other side of the mountain, only 18 kilometers away?

Already in the Middle Ages pilgrimages happened mainly spring time. When the nature wakes up, so it wakens also people's desire to travel. At that time traveling as a amusement was not known, pilgrimage was the way you satisfied your hunger for traveling. Pilgrimages could be called the Middle Aged charter trip, because people searched each others company and entertained themselves on the road, by telling stories, by singing, and eating and drinking.

The book, Canterbury tales, tells about a pilgrimage group, which received a mission from the owner of a guesthouse: everyone should tell two stories on the outbound journey and on the return journey aswell. The travellers were representing all the different classes, that existed at that time. A similar kind of phenomena you can see on the boats between Sweden and Finland. According a sociologist it is the only place where people can meet over the class boundaries in modern Scandinavia. Already at the middle age the going was quite wild on the pilgrimages. People were concerned about the young womens virtue. The normal people were more outspoken, and according a saying, the women left home as virgins and came back as prostitutes. I think this was exaggeration and was expressing more the mens desire to keep the women at home.

An interesting fact about prostitution and pilgrimage is that it was a bishop who owned all the properties where the prostitutes worked in London. Pilgrimige has alway being an important source of livehood for the church. Many documentaries have described different ways the church can earn money which modern pilgrimages are happy to pay. It is also true that the churches offers very cheap accommodation for the pilgrimages.

The churches have also protected refugees in many European countries so even this phenomenon is not black and white, like the most things in life. On my own, unholy pilgrimage, I did not visit many monasteries and churches. I stayed one night in a monastery in France and it was not a very nice experience. I came tired to the monastery and the priests did not want to let me in. After, looking for a booking a long time, I could show an E-mail about my booking that a friend had done from Rome. I was accepted men had to go to the mess and then eat before I could get a cold shower which I really needed after sweating the whole day. Well, I did not need cold shower but it was better than nothing. I was the only guest in the monastery. I was eating with the munks but I had reserved an table , where I sat alone and it felt very strange. One more peculiar thing happened. They served a can of beer to my dinner?! Hospitality or an excuse? When I write this I remember that it needed a confirmation by my friend in Rome, before the ylet me in. We easily forget unpleasant memories, at least I do. After that night I chose to stay in hostels and hotels. I could afford the hotels and wanted to show the people that not every pilgrimage do want to get everything for free. It is true that many people who can afford good accommodation do not want to pay anything. It gives the trekkers bad reputation and that is one reason why some countrymen let the dogs out, when they see people walking. Many hotel owners told me, how people like me want to have everything free. Most often it is people who have money, but take it has a hobby to try to pay as little as possible. I admit it is very expensive to trek for months but hey, it is voluntary. Needless to say that poor people cannot make journeys that takes months. What the hotel owners did not like, was the attitude pilgrims have. They expect that they are treated like poor people and they should get free food and accomodation aswell. The fact, that they are not poor, and the hotel is not doing charity work make the whole thing a bit peculiar. Monasteries and places like that have their own policy. Many has a policy according to which the guest decides how much money he/she wants to donate for the staying. Maybe the monastery I visited, knew that I was only one more cheating, rich middle aged man, pretending being poor? I was not and after that I used my money as a tourist should do.

I sincerely believe that the motives for the pilgrimage are more holy and personal nowadays than in the middle age. The modern people are maybe not so religious but they search more themselves and spiritual things than before. For many people pilgrimage in the middle-age was more like our traveling to the sun and beaches.

The most known pilgrimage route in Europe is Santiago de Compostela starts to remind middle-age, because the number of trekkers is so big, hundreds of thousands walk longer or shorter parts of the route.You can call this mass tourism.

Remote longing was known by me already before school time. I spent long times near the Europe nr 4 road and was wondering where the people were on their way, what kind of a feeling was there between the people, how their lives and relations with other people were, what they did in their lives etc. The stories of the people fascinated me already as a child.

With the help of books you can travel to foreign countries. You can also travel with different kind cf company, aswell as the ways of traveling can be many, why not on the back of an camel, or climbing a mountain. I think books can satisfy our need to know different people and places. It is good to be curious. The same curiosity is the most important thing for even the scientists. There is a very well written book about this curiosity and it`s significance. It is all about how important it is to be curious and have only abot 60 pages. I wanted to translate it to many other languages but the author do not want it to happen. His point is that the point will be missed, when translated to another language. I do not believe this but I have to respect his opinion. Anyway, the little book is fascinating. So simple and so brilliant; be curious!

It seems to me that a part of human constitution is the longing somewhere. It is very seldom I live just in this moment. I often plan different projects or think about the bad things, that happened in my life. Asian martial arts have helped me a lot, many get it from the nature. I do not believe that long meditation is necessary, it is not even good for the blood circulation. I witnessed the young peoples agony in China, when the children were forced to sit hours along the road, where we westerners were transported to the famous Shaolin monastery. We were from 63 different countries so the transport took time. I train meditation every day, mostly moving and also mental training and it suits me but many of my students get their power and relaxation from nature, I try to do my tai chi outside as often as possible. Even the old masters tried to avoid cities and preferred training in nature.

Respect

You need curiosity and a genuine interest when you travel, but also a certain amount of respect. You should respect not only the people you meet, but also the culture, the habits in different countries, even the local food. The way people clothes themselves in various social context is also different. This comes often as a surprise, or many not even detect that they made something funny or offending.Many scandinavians get bad treatment by service personal in restaurants, because local people think that they are not respected due to too light clothes at restaurant. An interesting difference is how different countries accept or not, the headlights in daytime. I have never heard an explanation, why it is so different but I respect every countries choice. I understand that even on a sunny day the headlights may make you more visible but why to forbid them? Can you get blinded by them? Whatever is the objective truth, I prefer not getting in troubles with the local police and maybe end up paying penalties.

I remember still very clearly, when the pilot made an announcement before we landed in Kula Lumpur 1989. " Dear passengers, Malaysia has a death penalty for drug offense. Please, get rid of all the drugs you have on you, even though you have bought them legally in Your own country. Take also good care of your luggage, that nobody has access to them. Thank You".

Respect is not the same thing as acceptance. When Malaysia wanted to have different lines in shops for women and men, I thought it was stupid. There are a lot of totalitarian countries which are interesting to visit but everyone has to decide if they want to visit the country or not. I have especially hard time in really poor countries, who even do not respect human rights. This book is not the right forum to discuss this problem, but naturally you can argument for both ways to react. Before olympic games, a common argument was, that democracy would increase because more westerners visit China. I do not think this happened but what is the alternative? Naturally you should even take care of your own personal safety. In some countries it is more urgent than a moral point of view.

Moral indignation is easy to understand but it can also hinder learning new things. Even though many things can upset me in foreign countries, I try to understand what is it all about. This is not invented by me, it is a normal way to relate to things in science. I believe that by understanding things you can also influence them if necessary. Moral indignation does not lead to a change. Before you become accepted as a indoor student in tai chi, everyone has to make a ritual, where we also promise that we do not criticize other tai chi schools or martial arts, because we do not know them well enough. In our own group we are encouraged to criticize because it is part of learning. This initiation rite was banned a long time in China, because it was considered as reactionary, but it has been taken back as part of the school tradition in many places.

Even the tourists who visit our country has to cope with our rules and ways to do things. I found it especially hard to explain my foreign guests, that they could not drink alcohol when eating lunch. The same thing is that on sundays there is no place to buy a bottle of wine in Scandinavien. You can go to a restaurant and drink it there, but you are not allowed to take it with you. There is simply no place you can do it. In a way the differences make the world a more interesting place. It would be quite boring to have a world like Disneyland. There are even places where rules against drinking are very strict and the consequences can be harsh, so read the information so you do not to have to stay 5 more years in the country you visit.

Once the local newspaper wrote an article about me in Malaysia. The newspaper has about 10 million readers so we decided to celebrate. I still smoked sometimes at that point and I wanted to smoke and drink a beer. That was forbidden but I was served the best food I eve had had and it was a fascinating and exotic experience although I did not get what I wanted. We were eating with hands, of course after washing them, and it was also a new, pleasant experience for me.

In Scandinavia have the midsommarparties been a terrifying experience to many. The big festivals can be frightening with a lots of alcohol, some englishmen told me that they had thought that it was the hell they had entered in. It can be hard to respect people and their way of life in that kind of situation.

The knowledge is always a good thing. My twin daughters were teaching dancing in South Africa and they were invited to have a dinner with a local family. The father of the family asked what the girls did want to drink, and they said coke. Afterwards, they heard that the family had to starve a couple of days because of the expensive coca cola bottles.

In a film from Iran, the women had enormously fun on the mens expense. They made the man believe that he decided everything, but actually the women were in control. These women used burka but were not stupid because of that.

I was once in Greece with my children. I used to talk with a swedish man who had children in the same age like mine. We had our parking places next to each other and we met there or at the pool bar. He was complaining about everything that had with Greece to do. I wanted to ask him why he had travelled away from his happy and lucky homeland and paid so much money, if he was not pleased with anything. I think that it is ok to see the things as they are in a foreign country, like stand up comedian Ismo Leikola does. He gets even local people with him, and they can see the funny things what he discovers, like silent letters. Ismo means that slent letters are totally an unnecessary thing but silent numbers! That would be great. Paying back your loan you can claim that the zeroes do not matter, because they are silent. I wonder what a bank says. He is astonished that the bank pays bach the money to the state. The state has an army the bank sends only letters and can back it up, with a cleaning lady or two. He says that Zhingis Khan had asked his 30 000 archers to be ready, if the bank had sent him a letter. He means that the bank would not insist to get their money back in that case. It would a conflict of intrerest, as it is called on high level of diplomacy.

Sometimes different behavior is wrongly interpreted as lack of respect. When Scandinavian people use shorts in a restaurant or when a French man contacts a woman he do not know. If he is interested he finds out her name and telephone number and in the north women interprets this as sexual harassment.

Behavioral pattern can also be quite comical. In many countries you say cheers in the beginning of the meal but in Sweden it is a use that they suggest toast several times. In many countries this means that you are very interested in alcohol and that you have probably been drinking before the meal.

Open and respectful attitude is enough. We do not have to have a degree in traveling. There is for example no need to inform everyone about the place you visit, even though you have been reading everything about the place. Woody Allen has made a funny section in his film where the film took place in Paris. A man with a minor role begins every meaning, " If I remember right so..". This is probably the same type of a person who does never stop playing guitar at a party.

The paradox of traveling

Traveling or mass tourism is a phenomenon which destroys itself. Spain is visited by 60 millions tourist every year and the number of Spanish people is 40 million. If you apply the same figures in Finland, it should mean that we would have 7 million tourist. I wonder if it is possible to be interested in every tourist? There is no time. The climate change probably makes the rich people to move to Finland. After 50 years we have estimatef 50 million inhabitants instead of 5 million. Our grandchildren are propably working on beaches selling and hiring all kinds of beach and sun related fun products etc. I have hard time to imagine a situation where a Finnish man says to a tourist " The best price for you, my friend". I think it goes fast to adjust to the reality which surrounds you, you have to.

It is hard to have respect for each other when the amount of travelers reaches too high level. Mallorca is a god example of this. They continued to build more and higher hotels and in between the hotels only restaurants and junk for the beach and souvenirs. In the end of the day it became too much exploitation. They had to break down some of the big hotels and build more human size of hotels with parks.

The big tourist places are often not nice anymore. Everybody should find their own place. You have to be independent and it takes time and money but the reward is big. Santorini was once a place for writers and painters but now there is even an airport. The sunsets are still fabulous but the time is over when there was mainly locals and it was an authentic place where artists with their way of living were deeply despised.

This is a paradox because at the same time every country wants to have tourism. Venice is maybe a good example that some kind of regulation is needed. The local people hate tourists and they are too many but it is up to the city and government to do something.

A Finnish writer and admirer of mediterrian culture, Göran Schildt, told in a documentary that his respect for mediterrian culture did not diminish, even they got enemies on a little island they bought a house on. With time they also found friends. I am aware that everybody can not afford a house in

Greece but we have to do something with mass tourism.

There are maybe not a quick fix to a growing traveling. Sustainable tourism is not possible with hundreds of million visitors in one country. Maybe to invest in so called modern humanists can be a part of solution. This is not a book about how to solve problems with tourism but I want to explain what the concept, modern humanists is about. It is an interesting idea.

AirBnB – How an hippie idea could lead to impoverishment of European cities

AirBnB was one of the most fantastic ideas invented in the field of travelling. People who like to learn to know new cultures and people can stay in somebody`s home, see the city and country with the eyes of an aborigin, get cheap accomodation and the host can earn some money, instead of multinational chains of hotels. Next time the roles can be changed, host can be visitor and vice versa. Maybe they even become friends, but that is not the point. With other words almost a hippie like idea for experienced travellers, who has a genuin interest of learning new cultures and people. What happened? Many of the beautiful big cities in Europe, especially citycenters, have been too expensive to young people to buy their first litte flat, even renting has become too expensive. Sometimes a bunch of friends have managed, together, to rent in the city, but the owners have doubled the rent and got rid of the local youngsters and, of course, made AirBnB of the flat. Guardian has interviewed people in Barcelona who are professional people, earning good money, but who are planning to move away from the city, because they cannot afford living in the city anymore. It is not a surprise that locals want to reclaime their cities. This is also connected to the fact that many cities have simply too many visitors.

I was managing an AirBnb in Zurich and discussed this issue with a dutch lawyer, my client. He believed that a legislation is not an answer, as I do. His point is that people always find a way to go around the legislation, if there is enough money to make.

Modern humanists

Modern humanists are people who have done everything and started to be interested, how the people in the country they visit, actually live and think. This group is going to grow, especially if there is a political will to support it. Sun, beach and cheap wine is still going to interest a majority of people. I discussed this with a pizzeria owner in Northern Italy. He lived in my mind in a country that is not so cold but he told me that when his vacation starts, he drives until he reach the sea. Northern countries did not interest him, they are cold and expensive. Sun, beach and party are always going to be interesting.

Modern humanists are interested in things many people think are boring. It can be learning how to make local bread, a promenade in a forest, to take a sauna bath, to discuss how long time you can be at home after you give birth to your child. Everybody does not need sky diving or bungy jump.

2014 I was working on a little island with a tourist group for a couple of days. The visit started with a info about the island and it was both facts and legends. At the same time we could taste the specialities of the island. Everybody forgot the rough boat trip on a stormy sea and we continued with tai chi in the sun. After training the visitors took a sauna bath and that waited a dinner with more local specialties on the menu.

 The stars are clearly visible on this remote island, where are no lamps or other light resources, so you can lie on the ground and check where the star formations lie with help of a map. Another nice memory is from Toscana where I worked as a voluntary. A group of Australian people learned how to make local pasta and I had the possibility to be part of that and cook with the guests. It was interesting, a local lady about 70 was the teacher and afterwards we consumed our handmade pasta and local wine. It was a fantastic way to be together and relax with people who you did not know. There are not many ways that get people so relaxed than cooking together and learning something new.

Every traveler knows that time makes the memories more pleasant. You can tell them to your friends, especially after a good dinner and strong red wine or on a cold winter night, in front of a fireplace, maybe with a good glas of brandy in your hand

The worst experiences become the best stories. I went to Reutling, Germany 2002 for a week to train. I thought that I could sit in the sun in the afternoons and drink coffee. These moments, contemplating in a cafe, makes the hard training easier. Especially after three days of training the learning gets heavy and difficult, your body and mind is overloaded and you need some moments that are relaxing.

I was unlucky to come there when the winter was the coldest in fifty years. It was below minus 30 and there was no heating in the place I was living. The place had been workplace canteen of a factory. Normally the winters are not so cold in southern Germany, so the windows gave me a good ventilation I did not need.

I was shown a place I could place my sleeping bag , because there was a warm water pipe under the floor. I slept with gloves and a stocking cap. In the morning I put the owen on and opened the hatch. I put my chair near the owen, almost in the owen and when it was warm I sat on the chair and warmed my feet in the owen. I did not freeze when I was sleeping but the mornings and times for a shower were terrible.

The coldness did not matter during the training, actually it was in a way easier to train in coldness compared to practise in a very warm place. The only problem was the moment after training when you took a warm shower and you should step out and the cold air was striking you. There was no time to get dry, basicly I put my clothes on right away and I crawled into my sleeping bag.

The third day I walked into the city and went to a cafe. I could not anticipate what would happen.

In the cold, the body is tensed all the time and when I sat in a warm and gosy cafe, with a steaming cappuzzino and a fanzy cake, reading a newspaper, I relaxed and......fell asleep. When I woke up I still had hard time to stay awake. This was my only visit in town, I decided to rest in my sleeping bag or I used the time filming myself doing the new material I learned.

Why did I not choose to take a cheap hotel instead? I do not recall how my thinking was at that point, but I think I thought that I get more rest by sleeping in the training place and I spare some energy by not having to walk very early to my daily practise and then very late in the evening back to the hotell. Then stinginess was surely one reason. I had already paid for the accomodation, it was included.

The Asian experience

I have been writing in martial arts magazines during decades. I wrote reviews about MA books, videos, interviewed interesting teachers and sometimes I wrote about my own experiences as a practinioner when travelling in Asia and elsewhere. Especially Asia was untill the beginning of the ninetees an exotic place, where ordinary people från Scandinavien did not travel except in their dreams. Nowadays it is only one of the places people plan to go on their vacation or travel with back pack, staying maybe a longer time before settling down and starting to have a normal, nine to five life. One editor in chief told me, that he begun to miss his youth and travelling, training or competing, after reading my stories. I am very proud of that comment.

Naturally I did not tell everything in the MA magazines. I did not lie, but I excluded the hardships, if possible. The truth was, that my first journey to Asia to train, was a disaster in the beginning. The plan was, that I would pay my accomodation by taking care of the dojo, training place. Do the cleaning every day, put the training devices back where they belonged in the evenings and many other things. I would sleep in my sleeping bag in the training place and even be able to pay part of the tuition by working. When I arrived, after travelling almost 24 hours, there was no room for me and there was no training place (dojo is often used as a name of a training place but it is actually japanese.)

I was so tired and disappointed, that I did not feel grounded. I actually did not feel the ground under my feet and I had been reading about what it ment. It is considered as a clear sign that your mental balance is seriously affected. I could not afford to go elsewhere to train, not even to buy a ticket home. Everything was sorted out and became good after couple of days. I got excellent tuition from my master, sometimes in a storeroom, sometimes in a field and quite often in my masters living room. For me it was only exotic and esoteric, so I was happy. The main thing was to get good quality tuition? I also got a little room in a warehouse, where I had company of bedbugs. I am not ready to tell more about that experience yet. I have to wait a little more, before it becomes a good story.

Armchair travelling

Planning of a journey and the time you are looking forward to get to the road can be very pleasant, sometimes the best part of a journey. When you sit comfortable in your armchair with a cup of warming tea, you do not suffer of too cold or warm weather. You are not hungry or tired or irritated. On the map, that is spread on your table, in front of you, obstacles, like the Apennines and the Alps are a piece of cake. You pass them easily and without effort, no matter if you are walking, bicycling or driving a car. You can take nice photos on the mountains and in your livingroom there is no rain or stormy weather that takes you with a surprise. There is no sudden wind, blowing dangerously hard and coming from nowhere, and which weather report said nothing about.

For example when I was walking to Switzerland from France, totally exhausted in the mountain and thought that I had made it, the only person I met that day told me, that I had only done the half of the climbing. I wanted to cry but managed to come to the top, before the daylight disappeared. I was very happy and proud of myself. A nice couple, owners of the hotell de France, were treating me well and for a change I got good food and good conversation. It was very rewarding after a long lonesome month in the north of France, which is a depressing place, with closed industry and empty houses after people who have moved away. The villages are becoming ghost like places, without even a cafe.

If you are going to visit a big city, so with a map it is easy. You plan to visit the places, that are a must the first time you visit a new city and you can plan one own place to visit, outside the tourist areas aswell.

In reality, only to visit one place a day is enough, with all the transfers in the city and queuing for the tickets and security controll. I prefer to use my time at a cafe and observing the people passing by. It is the theater of the streets. It is also good for tired legs. Your legs will get tired moving around in a city holiday. It is all included and gives a good appetite.

One rainy summer, working very hard, was saved because I had booked a journey to Greece with some friends, in the end of the summer. Every time I got depressed of the weather or working actually too much, I thought about Greece and everything felt much easier. The actual trip was really pleasant, even though it started in a bad way. I had worked from friday afternoon to sunday evening without any stop and was driving car to the airport, when dig forced me to drive 40 km an hour instead of 140. We became hungry as hours passed, but we ignored all the restaurangs that had open all night. We decided together, unanimously to eat when we arrived to the airport. Well, all the restaurangs were closed, not even fast food was at hand. We had to wait for the breafast time and it was a little bit difficult be happy and relaxed, when you are tired and hungry.

In an armchair we are calm, dry, happy and do not get irritated at small details that are not making our lives comfortable. We can ignore them and be cool. I think it is our right to enjoy travelling in an armchair. It is our right, even our duty. People who take the right to dream are more creative and more easy to deal with.

According to modern science, armchair journeys can be seen as mental training. If I can imagine a perfect journey in my mind, it will guide me in a real situation aswell. The contrary is true also. If I am afraid about all the bad and dangerous things which can happen, or what can go wrong, I am programming my brain to make it happen.

Naturally everybody must take care of themselves and be conscious about less pleasant things that can happen, but it is morea question of common sense.

Maybe all inclusive is so popular because of the security, you do not have to worry about anything. For me it is more like a prison but I maybe should try it once, before I can say anything. One thing is sure about all inclusive travelling. The local restaurant and bar owners have told me that it kills the natural competition between different places and the people do not go anywhere from their own hotell. everything is there, what ever they need. I think it is a sad phenomenom. It is not only a sad thing for local people but also for the visitors, it limites their possibilities to experience and maybe learn new things.

The importance of travelling to severability and detachment

The feeling of severability should be known to everybody, at least for those who are not travelling in big groups. If you travel alone with light bagage, you certainly have these moments when you feel that you are totally outside the life that is going all around you. Everybody are in a way ripped of the normal connection with his/her surroundings and the people living there.

I do not normally think about my social network but in my normal everyday life it makes life easier when you can phone your family, friends or some work mate in case you get troubles for example with your car. Almost everybody are using their realtives, friends etc when they get problems with the computer. It is interesting that with computers and internet connection problems we assume that somebody helps us for free. I do the same, I ask for help of every younger person if it is a computer related problem and I am not offering to pay for it.

Anyway, when travelling you do not have the access to the network, you are momentarily without it and it can be also a positive thing. It can liberate you and it will because you are temporarily free of the requirements and obligations of everyday life. We also assume that we are expected to do a lot of things and feel the pressure of it. We oushld welcome this momentary liberation of all responsibilities.

Many people experience severability and detachment as extremely constrictive. This is the reason why many fill their travelling days with more activities than when they are working normally.

Americans and Chinese are masters of this. A big city's all the ten most important attractions are visited in one and a half hour, included taking photos and the transport with bus from one place to another. It cannot be many minutes per attraction. This timetable according a documentary made in Stockholm. The timetable is verified but it still seems for me to be impossible to do.

When you realize severability and detachment in a context of travelling, they can give you and your own thinking time and space. Although the people all around us are hurrying somewhere, to work, to meetings and to take care of their own important things, you are totally an outsider. You can reach the outside world and your electronic bubble where ever you are with some device, mobile phone, ipad or lapptop but the stress and demands of everyday life are not present. You can stop time if you want and are brave enough to do it. Maybe you learn to limit the time used with social media. It is good to live in the real world. One TV and filmcritic used to remind people of the button in TV that shuts down the device. He said that he is obliged to watch all the nonsense but his readers are not. The same button exist in smartphones etc. I remember the excuse an italian teacher in Filipino martial arts had, when he told me that he did not be able to teach me, because he was working with his web page to sell his services? I was ready to come from the other side of Europe and pay him for teaching me, but the webpage was more important!

To do nothing is very important if you want to be creative. When I had three mobile phones because of work, and the fourth was my private, I did not write books or filmed documentaries. I think doing nothing, is a necessary prerequisite to be creative. So called laziness, for example sitting at a cafe table is not to be lazy. You need it to relax and get focused and let your energy to be gathered when you are not creating. I met a a professinal musician who told me that when he keeps his workshops all over the Europe, he tells the becoming symphony orchestra musicians to live and fill their brain with different kind of stimuli. He believed strongly that your creativity is not going to reach the highest possible level, if you are a musician and you use the limited free time to discuss the optimal angel of your hand and your instrument.

The dirigent of London symphony Orchestra, Esa-Pekka Salonen says that people think he is grazy, when he after working only wants to eat good food and have some wine. The most of the people would like to visit exciting places, parties, art galleries etc. Anyhow the energy is not unlimited. At a cafe table I can dream and think and listen. I have heard an actor and director have their first meeting about a planned film. Naturally I stealed parts of the conversation, especially cool sayings or truthts about acting and directing. A writer called Claes Hyllinger has made sitting in cafees to an artform. He wrote an short story how he was sure about that the family next to him was from France, then he listened more carefully and changed the country five times more. He never learned to know the right nationality. Sometimes I continue my childhood game and I wonder why people meet, how is their relationship etc.

The same author who tried to guess the nationality of the family tells in a short story how he had enamored to a waitress in Paris as a young student. There is a theory that claims that all our decision leads to different lives and all these different lives we choose are going on at the same time. In the reality we know the writer did not ask the waitress to go to the cinema with him. In another reality he is brave enough to ask and they become a couple. They move outside the Paris, get two children and the writer welcome everyone to their house if somebody is passing by.

I am not always thinking this kind of deep or strange thoughts, mostly I stare and only exist without thinking anything special. To get boared is important. If you are active all the time, you can not be creative. It does not matter what you do. The quality what you do beside creating does not have any signifinance, almost the contrary. Travelling can be one way to have boring time.

One very succesfull dance choreograhner, a former dancer, said in an interview that she could not work eight to five. She has to able to sit at cafees and wander around the cities she works in. It sounds somewhat an elitist style of life but it is good to remember that most of the time she works very disciplined and long hours.

To wandering around the streets had a name before, you hardly use it nowadays. I think that real walking in the city has to do with an interest in the history of the city, stories about the city and about the people living there. Architecture is a big part of the whole experience. As already many writers do, you can use walking as a way to do nothing or to have boring time. And at the same time exercise and let your brain get a rest.

Scandinavians seek the same by going to the country cottage in summer time, it can also be a boat or just a meditative walk in the forest. Scandinavian people tell me often how they load their batteries in the forest, to get renewed strenght. It could be my yoga teacher but it is ordinary people who have found a way to keep balance in their life.

Travelling and doing nothing extraordinary, or having boring time when travelling or at home can be a journey inside your most inner self. This I truly believe is necessary if we want to do any kind of creative work or actually art, or to feel balance and happiness in life generally. The artform does not matter, it can be painting, writing, singing, sewing. They all need the same freedom and energy, none is better tha the other.

The world of scents

The exciting world of scents needs it's own chapter. I admit that my own attitude is a bit too positive and romantic. The same scent or actually smell, which would make me sick at home, is exotic somewhere else. I take willingly deep breaths and feel happy to experience something new. I know that this is not an objective way to relate to the subject, but I do not care about it, I only enjoy.

At the University they teach you the U-curve about living abroad. In the beginning everything is exciting and new. With open senses we welcome everything we meet. Then comes the everyday life and it's problems and realities we have to face. We dip to the bottom of the letter U. Everything feels more difficult than back home. Then step for step we start to climb upwards and we start to feel better and the situation is hopefully in balance. At least we have a more balanced view on everything we meet, on a daily basis.

When we are travelling, we maybe can be on top the whole time. To live permanent in a foreign country cannot be compared with travelling. Even if you are travelling several months, it still is a different thing compared to living and working in a new environment. Anyway I know that my attitude towords scents has to do with this U-Curve.

The first thing that comes to my mind, when I think about scents is not, for example all the spices and food being cooked above open fires, at a nightmarket in Asia. It is not the Mecca of scents, the little town Grasse, nor metropolitan Paris, which has become somewhat the most important place for perfymes. I think about the fresh scent early in the morning, if this is blended with the wind from a lake or sea, even mixed with a smell of fish, that is even better. This is scent memory I am talking about is from Scandinavien, but you can get a bit similiar experience in Northern Italy, in the wintertime. You can almost feel the freshness and coldness in the white wine of the region. Maybe I am letting my fantasy too much freedom, especially when you know that I used to be a heavy smoker before, not for years now, but I think I lost part of my senses. They recover, little by little, but hardly all the way. It is although fantastic that the food tastes better every year, normally the process is the opposite when you get older.

I was working as a voluntary worker in Catania, Sicilien 2015. My walking path went through the fish market every day. I lived with an extreme low budget but I enjoyed my walking there, breathing in everything. It was a total experience with the sellers shouting loudly, a turkish tradition, I heard. It was always crowded so you had to adjust your speed with the visitors of the market. I was comfortable by the thought that I would buy excellent fresh bread for the clients for breakfast and I could also eat it, it was part of the deal. I love seafood and fish and I was wondering how I could enjoy walking there without being able to buy anything. Maybe it was all the colours of, for me, exotic fishes, seafood I know better. Anyway the deal was that I get no money for my work, but breakfast was included and accomodation aswell. Normally one more meal is included but here it was more question of using us volunteers as a free labour power, most of the time cleaning the toilets.

Afterwards I have been thinking about that time and I think that eating less than normal but not starving, heighened the feeling to be alive. I was writing really many hours after my work and I was happy to be able to concentrate, in the background the sicilian couple fighting every night. Downstairs was living the biggest mafioso of the city so in a way I was protected. Although I sometimes was lying aware, thinking what if somebody wants be the new capo? What happens then, they blow the whole building or do they only use weapons? I had to scamper through restaurants which had their tables on the pavement, also many shops had their products in the street. This way I was always reminded, that there was plenty of good food everywhere, but It was not for me. I was so happy to write in the beautiful, several centuries old house and apartment. I could also train there what I wanted, because the flat was big, reaching through the whole building, with two balconies.

My favourite place in every city is the market hall or halls, if it is a big city. Often I only visit them to watch and breath in everything. A tip for Barcelona market hall, walk through the whole place and find on the other side a place they sell seafood. Only locals go there, or mostly. They have good prices and excellent food. If you like colours take a plate of only seafood.

I would like to experience the magic, I experienced as a child. I think a big part of magic were that my senses were open to everything, colours, scents, voices, etc. Maybe travelling takes you a bit more near that world, where you could still dream freely.

I am convinced that it is possible to experience magic, the reason why we cannot is between our ears. According a rock musician tea and good company is enough to get a magical feeling of things. I am interested in it, because it has to do with creavity and is needed in arts.

Americans maybe mean the same thing in another context, if you smile to the world, the world smiles at you but if you smell.....

Slow travelling

Slow travelling is only one way to travel and is referring to slow food movement. It is not necessarily better or more sustainable than other ways but it has it's good sides. Surfers contend that they leave a huge carbon footprint, although their sport or activities does not affect the nature at all, on the contrary, the nature creates the conditions and possibilities. Here lies the problem because surfers travel a lot to find the perfect conditions for surfing. They travel all over the world and they drive car in their own countries and aboard searching for the best conditions to surf. Some surfers thinked about this and they changed their car motor so, they can use the oil that is used in hamburger restaurants for cooking, in their cars. This is an intelligent way to deal with this problem. The restaurants do not need to pay the fee for taking care of this waste product, it saves money for the surfers and is a little bit better for the environment too.

Slow travelling is maybe best for your own wellbeing. If you think about a week-end holiday in a big city, it is not necessarily a relaxing one. It can be it, because you maybe can get distance to your life and problems but it is quite stressing also. I am sure it is better to walk one week in nature if you want to calm down and maybe find some answers.

My youngest daughter came just back from Las Palmas with her mother, where they both had worked every day but they also took time to relax on the beach etc. Where can we put this way of travelling, in which archieve should we place it?

I think that a city week-end is a kind of road movie, where you are both the actor and director. You show the audience everything, how you are travelling, where you are heading, what you eat and drink and where etc, I think about the social media in this ontext. This is a lot of work and some delays of flights and traffic stockings takes some time too, so it is not relaxing, sounds like more hard work. Even I recommend not to use social media when travelling, it is very handy on a city week-end tour. You need information and you need it fast. That can make a difference.

When on trekking you should not use any devices to keep contact with everybody and everywhere. Take a real holiday from reporting everything you do. I had promised to write blog and articles in newspapers when I followed Via Francigena from Canterbury to Rome. One sponsor showed my position on their website and yes, it was partly a work for me. I was also updating my webpage and facebook, so I was more in the social media than in my ordinary life. I found only one book about the trekking I did and the writer recommendended also to leave the usage of internet and mobile. Well, she was also writing and taking photos like me, so I think she could not either live according what she thought would be an optimal way to walk long distances. I recommend the same, even though I cannot always do it myself. You will get some abstinence in the beginning but it goes over. Your near and dear ones, not to mention the cyber community manages a couple of days without you. You can send a postcard if you want to make people to envy you, or do like my friend, who is buying som postcards and then she goes and visits her friends after coming home, and gives them personally to everybody. It is a smart solution, probably she can tell about her experiences at a dinner table, or over a glas of wine. That is creative acting at it's best.

You have to take care of your security and part of it is, that your family or somebody else knows about where you are or where you should be. I got lost in Italy, all of sudden I found myself with a bicycle in the middle of a forest and the terrain forced me to carry my bicycle. When I finally admitted to myself that I did not know where I was and put on GPS with a planned route, done already the day before, I could easily take me back to the right track. I thanked the modern technology, but it is good to remember that it does not function everywhere. Many forget this in a boat and in mountains. The devices should also be recharged when you need them. I had with me resarcher, that I could use even without electricity, in the forest.

Travelling alone

For many only the thought of travelling alone is obnoxious and maybe also frightening. It would be too easy to say that it depends on your own attitude.

I have often missed company, especially when it is guestion of months of travelling and on locations there are few people living.

When you do not know if you should go left or right, it is easier if you can share the responsibility of decision making, and maybe look at bad decision more from an other perspective, maybe even humorously and have a good laugh when you find yourselves on a muddy field, instead of a nice, dry path in a beatiful forest.

I also missed company in the evenings, I should have wanted to share the experiences made during the day, especially if something unusual had happened. Only such a thing, like to share your dinner would have been nice, especially when the meal was extraordinaty good, as it often was. You can find excellent food everywhere in mediterrian area at lunchtime, and it is cheap.

There are also many good sides in travelling alone. You can choose your own rythm in everything, how fast you want to travel, where and where to stop. If trekking how long way you want too go in a day and you are free to change depending how you feel in your body and mind. You do not have to compromise where to sleep and what to eat. You can also more easily get contact with other people, even a couple is already an entity that is harder to approach and have contact with. Your own attitude is important in this matter, you have to have an open mind and really want to talk with people, it does not matter if you are a member in a big group, a couple or alone.

The best thing with travelling alone was that I had to find out if I was able to be alone a longer time. The value of that time spent alone started to reveal to me after couple of years from the actual journey. I became more self-confident, I began to trust myself that I could solve every problem I would meet, when travelling or in life in general.

I believe also that you cannot have a good relationship with someone else if you cannot be alone and like yourself. When you manage to do that, then you are ready for a relationship, instead only fullfilling the societys demands to build a family with Mother and father, two children, own house and a car or two. I was actually terrified the first time I should travel alone a longer time. When I was in Ireland and training for several months I really suffered,

 that I did not have any company or social life. That became better the next time I was there and I had also another way to relate to things, I wanted to see more of the country, the green island, not only train. When I was bicycling in France along a sad, empty landscape and villages I was really lonely. I could so little french that I could not communicate freely with people, if I happened to meet somebody. I remember that I was almost bitter when I got company in Italy which was the fun part of the trekking. I would have preferred to say that I made the whole Via Francigena alone. I do not think like that anymore. Actually I am happy now that I got the opportunity to experience both travelling alone and then with two friends and finally couple of days together with only one of my friends.

What I found out was that I can be happy alone and travel alone but I became conscious that I prefer to share my life with somebody, but I do not want to be alone in a relation. That is worse than being alone or solitude. English language can make a difference between solitude and loneliness. In my language this is not possibel, the same applies in many languages. The strange thing is that even though we do not have the word, many choose to live alone nowadays, it is a choice and active conscious decision, not a failure to find somebody. Your friends and family maybe want to see it like that but things change, little by little.

It is good that I do not suffer being alone, because a writer has to be able to be alone. My idea of being alone with your thoughts and work is, that it is a privilege. I have the luxury to create my own world, instead of fullfilling the company ideas and values which necessarily are not Yours at all.

Sometimes I go to a cafe and can concentrate really well in a busy commotion, if there is a moment that I am not writing all the time, I observe people and enjoy it. I have chosen to go to place which are not so noisy. I prefer the places that look like they used to look like 50 years or hundred years ago. They are more human, comfortable and homey. Maybe I am only getting old, but I do not like the places you are like on a stage, open space or windows from floor to the ceiling. It is like being in a public place, playing a social role, a social activity, look I am here, all the lights on me. You are there to be seen.

I want to read newspapers, write, observe people and enjoy the environment and all the fabulous sweet things they serve. It is good to be with people but not on a stage. I have got the best ideas for writing on cafes, aeroplanes and on trains. Partly it has to do with, that you cannot find an alternative activity, you have to sit where you are. Partly I think, it is due to other people give you more energy and inspiration. All the writers seek for a tranquil place to write but nobody can write in a vacuum. You have to live and interact with people to have something to say. This is the reason I have had more than 40 different jobs. I have had the privilegium to see different working environments and working conditions. It affects the people who are working there. For example when I was working in harbour I had to call a number 5 am, and there was this machine that with a metallic voice was repeating a lot of numbers. I had a number and if my number was mentioned I had work that day, if not I could go back to bed and sleep.

To be alone a longer time, for example walking, can help you to solve problems, although you do not get the feeling of a big solution, Heureka while walking. It does not happen like in a Hollywood film, where you get flash backs of your life and troubled situations in it and of all a sudden you are a new human being with new values and ideals. But do not worry, the mind is a powerfull tool and if you give it time and space it will help you.

I Could not always see my actions as a rational behavior during lonely days and nights for example when trekking through Europe. I was often swearing and thinking, why a reasonable logic person can do so stupid things and pay a lot of money for that too. Maybe the time has healed many things but after been writing about my pilgrimage in several books and my photo exhibition has circulated around the country and people have liked it, I have start to value my experience. As I mentioned before, the value lies also in a higher self esteem, many fears have disappeared and I have started to value people more and cooperation with them. I make my decisions in life without fear and anxiousity. I also think that if you do not choose, it is also a one possible choice.

I imagine that everybody could profit to travel alone and without being all the time in contact with everybody and actually with nobody, through the social media. Maybe people could get a chance to experience unity, when being alone, instead of making yourself busy even on vacation. When you concentrate on your next step, you can stay calm, confident and trusting. We do not worry what happened yesterday and what is going to happen tomorrow. We only take the next step and it is enough.

The philosophy of failure ang getting lost

I have found the most interesting places and experienced the most special things by getting lost or that have had to make route changes because of an minor accident or encountered problems with the equipment.

I was bicycling down the mountain, feeling free and powerfull in the sunshine, near the swiss boarder in France. I had had a free ride for several kilometers down the hill when my tire broke. I was vexed, why should it happen now when I was feeling so good and why was the bicycle shop still closed when I left my latest stop over. I actually had fixed my tire the day before there, and had decided to get extra tires and equipment to fix problems with the bicycle before I continue my journey, but because the shop was closed, when I left, I had nothing to fix my bicycle with. More than one month without any problems and then two days in a row?. I had deserved to enjoy my ride after working so hard and so long time. This was the way my thoughts went round in my mind. I was leading my bicycle down the hill and after only fifteen minutes I came to a little village. There was nobody in the reception in a liitle hotel by the road so I continued to the centre of the village. I found a place they repair bicycles, left my bike there and checked in the town hotel next door.

I started to feel better and I took my camera and went out. My emotional state was more balanced and I started to notice that the village was very pittoresque. I had an espresso in a cafe opposite a park where I saw a sculpture, which was interesting and familiar. I took my time enjoying the wonderful feeling you get after been on the road all the day and you finally can rest and enjoy life, knowing that you have a clean dry place where you sleep and you will get a good dinner before you get a good night sleep. It was not every day I managed to eat before sleeping. I took a closer look at the statue, it was made by Gustave Courbet, one of my favourite artists! I found out that I had come to his hometown by accident! He chocked the whole art world by making big paintings of ordinary people in the village of Ornans. A burial at Ornans made first the village people proud but because before, only people in power were allowed to be in big paintings, the critic was devastating. Village people turned against the former hero. He also painted the origin of the world, that still today would be forbidden in many context as too vulgar, pornographic or something like that.

I spent two days in Ornans, enjoying the tranquil atmosphere and autumn colours in the nature. His museum is located partly above the river. When you leave the building you see the the water under your feet through glas floor.

The road from Ornans followed the river, surrounded by mountains. There were no cars so I had a fantastic ride. I thought that Ernest Hemingway would have liked to fish there, waiting for the bottles of white wine to get the right temperature in the cold water of the mountain river.

When I really got lost in Apennines, my shortcoming led me to a place that was direct from a fairy tale. I had left Bologna and was climbing up all the time with my heavy equipment and bicycle. High up in the mountains I found this fabulous place with green mountains everywhere. I was lost and tired and I was thinking that I was hallucinating but I was not. I came to a little village and got tip of a hotel outside the village. They had recently opened and were keen to get people interested to come to their remote place. I was taken care realy well. After the experiences in northern France, I was in a paradise. The hotel Palazo Loup, near village Loiano is still in my heart. I have visited it afterwards and I hope to to visit them in the future. There was a conference at the daytime, but in the evening there were only two catholic priests and me having dinner in a centuries old part of the big building. I really enjoyed my stay and it was good to me to talk with the personal. We even checked prices, if I could bring people there to train chi. That has not happened, yet, but I still hope to share the place with many more. After a long bath and a good nights sleep I went for a walk and photographed the surroundings. The place was real even in the morning light and it still looked like a saga.

I had company during one weeks trekking in Italy. The second day with company, one of the groupmember of three people, got so tired that we did not get to the accomodation in time, before it got dark. One of the group members talked perfect italian, so we stopped in a cafe to arrange everything. The owner of the accomodation told us that it was impossible to find our way in the darkness and nobody could pick we up, so we cancelled our booking. We started to get a little bit worried. I was the only one that had sleeping bag and the nights were near minus already. The cafe owner was married with the mayor of the nearest city Orio Litta and we could find our way there and the mayor would wait for us there and accomodate us in the town hall for free. When we arrived to Orio Litta, all the men in the cafe were clapping their hands. They were having their aperitifs with the mayor and had heard who we were.

The mayor was a very nice and generous person. I was not used to this treatment, on the contrary.Some farmers let their dogs loose, when they saw I was passing. I think they believed that we damaged the nature and their fields. I have hard time to believe that trekkers are that kind of persons, of course there are always some rotten apples but why would you choose to walk weeks or months, only to get the chance to destry something? It does not make sense.

After we had the chance to wash ourselves and get dry clothes, the myor drove us to a nice little place outside the city. He was a big cycling enthusiast and told us that he could keep us company a couple of hours on our way to the next city Piazenca. I made a video interview next morning and got a cityflag as a present.

In the town hall we met two trekkers, who were on their way to Rome. They had a dog as company but the dog had big problems with it`s paws. I had been reading, before my journey, that pets cannot take the long trekking. I had smirked to that information but it showed to be true. Another thing with the dogs is that the local dogs has home ground so it is another problem.

When we woke up the english couple had left already, a bonne voyage note on the table was left, written of them.

We had happened to get totally lost the day before, first in the forest and ended up on a muddy fiels, where we met a farmer. Maybe they have right in the end of the day, the farmers. We had to clean the city hall, because our bicycles left a mess.

The mayor joined us and showed historical places, like where the middle age pilgrims had crossed the river Po, rested etc. We followed the river all day and could talk with the mayor, because there was enough place to bicycle side by side, two persons. We changed places . so all the day we could communicate with ease. For me this was fantastic, after being alone one and a half month. About noon the mayor returned back home and we continued to the next city. My company had a short vacation, so we chosed a nice trattoria and had a good lunch. I was watching the group of men who had bicycle clothes still on. The had apparently done their exercise and were now enjoying wine, food and good laughs.

Afte the lunch our way was blocked because of a middleage party. We were served warm wine and watched a parade with only middleage clothes and things they used to have back then. The man serving us wine tried to convince us that Via Francigena did not go the way we had been told. We tried to be polite and listen to him but I thinka nobody of us was so concerned about if the right track went two miles from where we did. It followed the safe route then and nowadays it is not always possible to follow it, so what?

These changes, failures, getting lost led to most interesting things. They also give strenght to trust in life and yourself, so that you can do what you want, although you are risking a failure. It also reduces the amount of worrying we all do, all the time. What did Bob Marley sing? Don`t worry...........

Unity- solitude or loneliness

The theme of unity was already touched in a previous chapter about travelling alone. We are able to feel unity with other people and nature or surrounding environment although we are alone. When crossing half of Europe I left one chilly, cloudy morning a little French community early in the morning. Mining was abolished and the community was in the process of degeneration and becoming deserted. Not a single open cafe was to found and I had to begin the day hungry and cold. I felt lonely and sad, even unsecure and weak. I was swearing my spontaneous and trusting attitude to things and fast decisions. I could have checked the day before that there is a place open or I could have shopped some breakfast already in the previous evening. I felt myself really lonely, as a little poor creature.

The motion of the body transformed this feeling to something else. After bicycling some time the body started to warm up and the endorfines started to flow. The stiffness of the body disappeared and the coldness, loneliness and misery changed to a feeling of warmness, security and joy. I had also entered in a beatiful forest of beech and I really enjoyed my ride in the nature.

I was one with the nature, with everything. I even got a good breakfast after one more hour on the road.

Well, this feeling disappeared later that day. After couple of hours pure joy the deep hills forced me to walk with the bike and ali my planning was gone, because after several hours of walking I had managed to make only a little part of the planned whole day's trekking. This kind of roller coaster of feelings and terrain was not the usual thing. Actually I had time already, still the same day, to experience a smooth couple of hours bicycling with easy terrain. In your everyday life things do not change normally so fast, but every and each one of us have our up and downs.

We are all alone in the end of the day. We have different ways to try to forget about it, working too much, drinking too much, maybe bicycling too much? It is like Emil Durkheim discovered that suicide is a social fact. It is part of human behavior. We try to keep death, loneliness away, like in Monthy Pyton sketch, where americans were annoyed, when death was knocking on their door. It was not an appropriate time. In martial arts is a way of thinking, or was, that you should be ready and prepared to die, partly because you live the way that you have no regrets. This is what Astrid Lindgren, the creator of fantastic literature said of this topic.

You should live in a way, that you are prepared and ready to die, when it happens, I think, tralla lalla la.

To plan or not to plan?

That is the big question in this context although we had maybe a bigger issue under our microscopes in previous chapter, so to speak. Needless to talk about all inclusive type of travelling in this context. I understand, especially parents of small children which are already overloaded with everything. They need all the help they can get.

For the rest of us is important to decide whether or not book accomodation in advantage, when trekking or actually independent how you travel. I travel normally outside the high seasons so even in countries where there normally are a lot of tourists, so outside the season finding an accomodation is not a problem.

When I visited an interesting area of New Forest in southern England, I heard a conversation between a couple and the reception personal. This was in the forest hotel near the village Burley and if you do not know it so cows and horses wander freely in the village streets and in the forest roads, so take care. Barley is also known for it's witches, but it is not my cup of tea but may interest quite a number of people. Anyway, it was already October and the couple were exhausted. They had been chasing a hotel room all the day. What they heard here was that the hotel and all the hotels in the neighborhood were fully booked for weeks to come.

Not even the willingness to pay for the most expencive suite did help.

If possible I try to be free and not to book accomodation. I know some people who trek for weeks and have booked accomodation for every night. What if you have to stop of some reason? You loose all the money for weeks of booking. You are not free. You can not stay an extra day, because you found a fantastic place you want explore more, or that you have to rest, your back or knees are hurting too much and it is torture to go on, and you risk a permanent injury. One thing I had to suffer because of this freedom, was that when I checked in without booking outside the high season, the room was not upheated. I had a sleeping bag but I met a Swiss man who did not have a sleeping bag and he told me that he had been trapped in the hotel room. He was so cold that his fingers did not function and he could not open the door. Once he had broken the key, because he lost his feeling in the fingers and used too much force.

By the way this man was the only person I met on my more than 2000 kilometer trekking, besides the couple I told about before, who was on the same route as I was.

The meeting happened early in the morning and it was still minus one celsius, so we could not chat very long time. We had to move on and I started already to think about Rome, and getting there fast. I wanted to end my journey, lie in the bath for hours, sit in the cafes for hours and watch people pass by.

Sleeping bag is good to have when sleeping in a tent, but also in hostels and hotels outside the season. I learned to choose restaurant, depending if it was warm inside. I remember one cold morning, north of Siena, Monteriggione. I wanted a rest and a coffee and to become warm. After ordering my coffee I saw locals had quilted jackets and I had thinn shell garment. I took my coffee in italian way, in one go and left. I found another place with local reconstruction workers. It was warm and cosy there and the food was better than normally. Yes, everywhere is good food in Italy, but this was better than average or maybe the cosy, warm place did it? Anyway, normally I avoided heavy food in the daytime, because bicycling became also heavy after heavy dishes. Now I needed it and thanks sitting there for a long time the sun had warmed the air and the rest of the day was pure pleasure, bicycling in the sun. I have never tried the alternative, where a company takes care of your luggage and transport it to your next accomodation. It sure makes bicycling more pleasant, without heavy thigs to carry and watch when stopping. You can also take more clothes with you, which is crucial when the weather gets colder.

If you plan to eat gourmet food, so even in the country side the best places should be booked sometimes more than six months before your journey.

The most freedom you can get, is to have your own tent, sleeping bag and own canteen. It is also the cheapest way and you are totally free. Naturally the weight and lack of comfort is present. On the other side, when you stop and have cooked your food and can lie down and rest in the nature, it really needs a three star restaurant and a five star hotel, to be better than that. When weather conditions are bad and if you happen to get wet, then everything is better than that.

For some is just the lack of comfort the thing. After missing the normal things for a while, you start to value basic things. Take a shower, buy a dish, take a bus, go to cinema etc is like really easy and a pleasure, instead of getting irritated if it takes one minute more than it should.

How to find good restaurants?

When you are travelling you do not find excellent reastaurants, they find you. There is an exception if you can afford three Michelin star restaurant, otherwise you have to be lucky. There is a rule of thumb that you should go to a place which is crowded by local people. I visited Santorini 2010, did actually not to want to go there, but got last minute price you could not say no to. We came to the little hotell late in the night and because the restaurant round the corner happened to have open, we had something to eat there. The restaurant had bare neon light bulpes in the ceiling without any cover, it did not look nice, it was flagrant and that is already un understatement. The owners were lovely people and we found out that the food was excellent and much better than in the expensive places with candle light on the tables, nice tableclothes etc.

The year 2013 I was living in Italy and had invited my children there with their husbands or boyfriends. We were 9 person and we hardly got place in a little restaurant on the Via Domenico Scarlatti, Al Buon Umore. The main courses were less than five euro and the wine was only couple of euros one liter. There was no menu in english and the personal did not speak english but what a lunch we got. Everybody were happy and satisfied and I was so lucky to be together with my family. For me it was un unforgettable occasion. It was maybe not so fantastic for my children but all seemed to be happy, at least in the photos taken then. My youngest daughter's boyfriend told us later that the restaurant was mentioned in Michelin guide. Partly the good feeling was due to the fact that everybody were on vacation and we had all the adventures in Milan still in the future, waiting for us. For me it is still an experience above the average. For me food is important and gives me a lot of pleasure. It is a total experience, which is best to share with somebody. What is the italians say about sin. The only sin you can do is to eat without company.

A quite big number of good restaurants do not even have a name plate that shoes where they are. The locals know without signs. I have seen it in Luzern, in Switzerland and outside Desenzano, Garda lake, there is a restaurant that even Taxi has difficult find. Only a stone wall in the middle of nowhere. No houses, nothing. When you go in, it is full of people and activities. Above fires are whole carcasses grilled slowly and waitresesses are hurrying across the tables. You get a bottle of house wine without ordering and there is one meny, you can of course choose not to eat everything but the cost is extremely low and the atmosphere is relaxing and unpretentious. You better love eating if you go there. I have to admit that I normally prefer quality instead of quantity but here the two meet and you end up eating way too much. If you want to enjoy your dinner in a discreet place, where people talk with low voices and the waitresses glide silently, serving you without asking to then this is not a place for you. Both the customers and staff speak loudly or shout but it is a warm and welcoming place, almost like a cliche of an Italian restaurant but I love it. The name of the place is Trattoria Cascina. You have to have a car or maybe you can bicycle but there is no streetlights, so maybe best to take your car or a taxi.

I think that naming good restaurants is stupid because they change owners and the best place, can over a night become the worst, even the opposite happens. Also naming restaurant, eventually results in that the restaurant has so many customers, that they do not have to care about the quality anymore. In Heathrowe there are a group of people testing the quality of food and service and by doing so, trying to counter the fact that restaurants are going to have a plenty of customer even they serve bad food. Michelin try also to help customers by constantly testing the quality. All this being said, I mention the latest favourites but please, do not come after me, if you are disappointed. There is a little place in Cisano, also Garda lake, eastern side, where the waitresses has to cross the only road passing the village every time they serve guests. The road is busy, even on low season. You can not miss it. You are sitting only a couple of meters from the water.

If you can afford to eat in the city of Desenzano go to a place called Colomba. It means an eastern cake. The owner is one of my teachers in Silat and owns the place with his brother. His parents and family visit the place everyday. If you say hello from me to Carlo you can order my speciality, pasta with seafood.

The italians like to bicycle round the lake. I would not recommend that. I tried once, on high season the western side and could experience what the guide books said. If you dare to bicycle there, you are never going to be afraid of anything anymore. It is near the death experience, literally. There is no place on the side of the road and if you lean a little to the left, well you do not have to worry about anything any more.

The price level in Desenzano is high and not necessarily the best food you can get. The fact remains, almost everywhere in Italy you get good food. There is a cheap place in Centro Commerciale de Vele outside Desenzano. If you can stand the notice in a very loud place you get interesting and good sushi on a conveyor belt. You will eat too much so book no activities after eating there. For ten euro you can get really exciting variations of sushi. Why I am mentioning these places I normally avoid? Maybe because there is also. quality, not only quantity.

It is good to remember that you choose what to eat and how much. I used to eat the whole menu but stopped and then I found a book, written by a finnish chef. Het old the same story in his book, that he kept on eating everything, primo, secondo etc during ten years, before he found out that italians eat what they want, there is no must to press all the dishes. Sometimes you get a lot to eat only to apero. I have got straw berries, pate, olives, cheese, hammon etc etc. and was actually not hungry when we went to eat.

I have to say in this context something about my experiences about food. I like to go to restaurant with professional and friendly staff. Although my heights in eating have been fresh fish, catched only a couple of hours before prepairing it to a dish. You only need fresh fish and sallad and you are in heaven.The biggest difference between the restaurant and food culture in different countries is the time spent and the distances travelled after a good restaurant, or for example to buy basic products for cooking.

I followed a language course in french, where a young french man, about 23, was interviewed. He tried to explain that he considered it normal, to drive more than one hour one way, to get a special chicken. The occasion was probably a quite wet evening, with friends and lots of wine etc. For us Scandinavians this does not make sense. The Scandinavian interviewer, of course, asked if it was worth it. The young man really did not understand why it was hard to understand.

I got a question once if I could think of going to eat out after having travelled all day to southern Switcherland from Sweden. Yes, they are different countries. Swiss people make the watches and dig tunnels through mountains. I answered the question with yes. I got mad when it showed to mean 1.5 hours driving on small, slippery mountain roads in one way. The food was good, but was it worth it? Yes, but not that day. Later I met a swiss couple, who both had high income. They used all their money on food and wine. This was in the french part of the country. I know most swiss people value sparing their money.

Voluntary work- one way to experience the world and stay longer times abroad

One prerequisite to voluntary work is that you have enough time, minimum three weeks but eventually even shorter time is possible.

It has been young peoples`s way to experience the world, but more and more older people, even retired people use this opportunity. Quite often the motive can be other than travelling. It can be a way to find permanent work in another country or to get a good picture of the situation in the country in general, and the labour situation especially. I have met people, who openly tell, from the beginning, that they want to have a real work and hope that voluntary work can help them to make their dream come true.

At it's best can voluntary work be a unique way to travel and to learn to know other people and cultures. Even the employers can travel by talking and changing ideas with people visiting them and get help with their business. At it's worst it is question of abusing or exploation, both ways.

Employers maybe only want to use free labour force or the voluntary workers want only to have a free vacation.

I have experiences from both sides, as a employer and as a voluntary worker. I got my contacts via an organisation called Workaway. The voluntary workers pay a reasonable fee and employers advertise for free.

I should collect olives and make wine, in a traditionell way in Toscana. There was no wine making, not even grapes. This was partly due to the weather but also because the owners did not care so much and their knowledge was almost non existing about wine making. They were very good in consuming wine. It was clear for me, that my function was to be a baby sitter to a man over sixty years old. His wife went away to work with the english speaking tourists and the man could not concentrate in anything more than fifteen minutes. He liked to drive car on the country side and visit restaurants and bars. I felt pity for my coworker Chris from Australia who wanted to make his last

Europa visit and study winemaking in small scale. His work in Australia was to grow the berries, not the wine making. Our hosts were also from Australien, actually the man was originally italian but had been living a long time in Australia. We both left the place before it was actually agreed, but the hosts did not care, there was not simply not enough to do. We did some work in the morning, finished it and drove around the Toscana, with my cabriolet, the afternoons and visited interesting places.

The male host in Italy did not like me because I sometimes smoked when drinking wine. He hated smoking. I even asked him why he was treating me differently, he liked Chris, the Australian guy. Anyway I left, first heading Sicily and the second biggest city, Catania. Chris went to Finland and lived well in good hotels, having some fun. I cleaned toilets in a hostel, trying to get my hosts to join me over a glas of wine, or dinner but I did not succeed. They did not want to have any cultural exchange, or eny exchange what so ever. They only used me and were indifferent. I was quite pleased with my stay anyway, because I got a possibility to live in a house, which was centuries old and interesting. My apartment went through the whole building with two big balconies. Downstairs was living the biggest mafia boss in the city and I also heard the voices from the bar located in the house and a local couple, next door neighbours, that were fighting all the days. The man was drinking and the wife did not like it, but sometimes they both said I love you and there was a moment of peace. I managed to write a book, a novel in that apartment, which was never published and I also translated one of my books about tai chi which was published and is really popular still, at this point after three years.

From Sicily I took a rent car to Bari and then Croatia. My car broke in Sicily and after three weeks it was prepaired but got the same problem again and everything begun from the beginning. I had to call the insurance company, wait for the tow truck etc. I could not wait for the reparation because that day I was leaving Sicily so the insurance company gave me a rent car for free.

In Croatia I finally got contact with local people and I did not have to clean toilets, I was teaching tai chi on a beautiful beach. Croatia is as beautiful as Italy but cleaner, cheaper and still at that time, not overexploited as their neighbour.

I have also been a voluntary worker in Finland for examle in a jazzfestival and in a filmfestival. These were really nice experiences. The midnight sun filmfestival was special. I had the honour to work as Peter von Bagh's private driver, he was already sick and they wanted me to work with him because I could maybe not to try to limit him, because of the illness, which he hated. He was at that time the artistic leader of Bologna filmfestival and was lecturing at many festivals and happenings all over the world. Unfortunately his illness won in the end but he was active writing and having new projects untill his death. When I met him first time he asked me to tell my story in three minutes while driving! I met him in Helsinki a couple of months before his death and he was very pleased when I told him that the festival had inspired me to make my own documentaries and write books more seriously. He told me that it was the basic idea behind the midnight sun filmfestival, to inspire people to create their own films.

I have also only positive memories of the jazzfwstival in Raahe, on the westcoast of Finland. I was building the area and also driving the musicians from airport to the festival area, hotel etc. I met Kekko Fornarelli and his band. I drove them around the city one day, showing museums, art galleries and the boys said that it was unusual for them. Normally they saw only hotel and festival area and airport. Kekko placed himself in front of a statue of our former president Kekkonen so that you only could see the word Kekko, naturally the rest of us took pics of this. I met him a couple of years later in Bari, Italy and we discussed my idea of a music film, hopefully different compared the normal standard, which is quite low and uninteresting for the public, only the hard core fans likes them normally. That is also a project undone, because I could not meet him as we had planned, the rent car company needed my car and I had to change my plans, once again.

My experiences as a voluntary worker are mixed. I was talking with a well educated finnish man in Sicily. He had only bad experiences with a start in Finland, where the boss made him cry. He had identified different types of companies using volunteers in a bad way as free labour force, hoping to get the business going better by not paying any salary to the workers.

I also invited volunteers to my camping and it was also a very mixed experience. Some of the volunteers had an open mind and were not afraid trying to work with different things, some started to play cards in the middle of working day and were complaining about the food. They wanted meat and we usually had sammon and other healthy food, a lot of vegetables etc. Many were too young and needed more parents than a employer and many could not even english, which was a absolutely a minimum, a must to work in a camping and hostel. One of the volunteers we took with us to our private parties and she became friend with our friends. That should be the case and I learned a lot only by talking with her.

I would recommend to make an agreement of two weeks time of work after that you decide whether or not to continue, this applies both sides equally. If things does not work of some reason a month is a long time to wait that the misery will be over. Be careful but openminded and try to give an honest picture how you are as a person and how is the work. To be bullied or wash the toilets does not promote the peace and understanding in the world. It is also good to remember that it is working, not holiday, you have to accept some toilet cleaning. I used to give my workers the rest of the day free when they cleaned the toilets. I arranged them a free gym and tennis court and they could borrow my car if it was available. After four goode experiences last year and one really bad, I would say that it is a must to talk with each other. If some part has not the time needed, something is wrong. If the employee is paying the travelling and giving one month of his/her life for free, the employer has to take it seriously. The last bad thing happened when a hostell cancelled two days before I should start working there two months. It can be avoide by having, skype, whatsup, some conversations. I m not going anywhere without that. Naturally, there are no quarantees but you can at least try your best. Read so much about the company as possible and if it is a family, contact the people who have been working there before.

I still believe that the idea is good behind voluntary work and you can become friends for life if you are lucky.

Coach surfers

The organisation Coach Surfers was established after second World War to contribute to the World Peace among all the nationalities. It functions so that after you have accepted to become a member, you can offer accomodation in your home for one or two nights or guidning in the area you live in. You can also ask everybody in the list, if you can get the same at their home. I met members in Florence and got a lot of information and a fun evening in the city. Nobody has been interested to come to my home but it is natural, because partly of the location up north and partly that I am registrated as a single man, terrible and dangerous by definition.

If you are a young person or/and a couple, you have much bigger chances, also if you live in Florence, London, Paris etc. They actually drown in applications. This is nothing to do about, only to accept.

The China syndrome

 One of my oldest students in Martial Arts has nowadays an own school of Kung Fu. We were training together and came to this idea that we compete for the each other, even we were not experts in the other's style. I would learn from him a simple handform which is different moves, kicks and strikes etc. I would also follow him to China to compete with that form. I would teach him tai chi sword and he would compete as my student. I do not know where we got the idea but I was thinking a long time, whether it was right to visit a country, where they did not respect the human rights. I decided to go and we headed to Asia. I remember the first morning when we were tired, the flight was eight hours delayed. All these chinese in the park training everything but chinese arts. We western people were the only ones practising Qi Gong, Tai Chi and Pakua, I was training mostly Hung Gar.

The second day we should visit the famous Martial art monastery, Shaolin. We could not believe what happened. The little chinese city, about seven miljon inhabitants was closed for our 63 different nationalities. The police had closed the roads so we could drive and pass the whole city without stopping. When the road started to climbing up to the monastery both sides were covered of children with munk clothes, sitting in a lotus position, with crossed legs. Mattias, one in our group told us afterwards, that the kids were crying of pain, having been sitting too long time in a position that did not allow blood circulation. We were served a show with internet projected on the mountain wall and young acrobats doing dance, gymnastics, juggling and maybe little martial arts. The next day we visited a place and there were Chinese TV and even international TV. One evening the chinese olympic committee served a dinner with a show, food and wine as much you could consume in one night. It was obvious that we were used as a tool, to get wushu as an official sport in Olympic games.

We were reserved an own guide, a girl who was studying english at the University. We were onlysix persons that she should controll.I asked her once about the polution that prevented us to see the sun. She told me that she does not know the word pollution.I explained that it is the thing, that prevents us to see the sun. When my groupmembers started to kick my legs, I did not press her any more. She was a very nice person and when the guys went to buy hygien articles and some stayed at the hotel, she had a problem. We solved the problem so that she could tell the taxi to wait outside the shop, so they were under controll all the time.

It still feels bad and disloyal to be critical to our hosts, after drinking eating and being entertained royally. The responsibility of our hotel was on a very stressed young woman. I always remember how this person, who saw bitter and hard, transformed into a beautiful woman, with a nice smile, when we left. She could finally relax after we were gone. It was maybe unwise to travel there, but it was an experience to be treated like a VIP.

At the airport when leaving China, we were first told we had to wait there days. Our flight was cancelled. When our chinese guide told the personal who we were, we were collected by a taxi, we were served good food and we had the possibility to use taxi the whole day as we wished, it was waiting for us. In the evening we were collected and flew home in first class with Lufthansa.

Travelling in cinema

There are cuntless of road movies but two are in their own division, Thelma and Louise and Mika Kaurismäki's Arvttomat, worthless.

I saw Worthless the first time when travelling somewhere. I became right away interested, there was something new here and at the same time a feeling of avantgard,french film in sixties. It is still my favourite road movie but of course there are many good ones.The fantastic world of film can transport you around the world, into the outer space, especially if you like Scifi. I do not like it but if a film is Scifi or not, it does not matter, it is upon the qualities the film has, not in which category, genre we can place it. Interstellar, to mention the latest I liked and Arrival from the same year. Then are the Classic based on the novel written 1961, Solaris, and also bladerunner with a young Harrison Ford. He is still chasing the bad guys but his hips start to be finished, I am afraid.

Road movies have often the same problem as music films, the format is more importaant than the contents. Mika Kaurismäki has done one more good road movie, Rosso, where the most famous scene is when an italian contract killer and a finnish man are singing in the car, while driving, sono italiano. All these films are bigger than life, as Peter von Bagh called his favourite films. Who needs life when you have got arts?

If you get the possibility so visit Orion in Helsinki. Only the building is worth visiting the place, and you can see quality film at half of the price you pay for mindless action films. I am afraid the decision is already made and Orion days are counted in the street of Eerikinkatu. It is going to move to modern building, new library, which cost us taxpayers more than the old fine building, so why this decision?

I was living on the other side of the road, opposite Orion and I was travelling a lot with films, everyday, sometimes up to three films in the same evening. I think it is always magic to lean comfortable back and enjoy watching a film, together with other people, it is magic.

Travelling by train is often shown in cinema. There are books written of this catogory of films, so I leave it, but the first publicly shown cinema was about a train coming to a station by Lumiere. It is said to have caused panic in the public, which I doubt, anyway the travelling by train is important in film history. It used to be the symbol for the modern world and it's technical revolution and hectic lifestyle, maybe it has lost it but the trains have something special. It is easier to start a conversation with people in train, compared with flying. Maybe it appeals us like boats, it takes some time but we accept it and actually get a short break from everyday life.

" Hobby traveling"

Many of us has a special hobby, because of which
they travel a lot. All kinds of activites where there
are competitions, travelling is a natural part of your
life. I have been competing, functioning like a judge
and trained longer or shorter times in foreign
countries. What comes to the amount of time,
learning more on seminars, training camps or simply
moving to live in the place a teacher is living, has
taken most of my time. Learning has been
everything from two days seminar to training on
whole time basis nine months.

In Ireland, Kilkenny, I have trained several times 2-3
months per stay. Yes, Kilkenny is also the famous
dark irish beer. The first time I practised 6-7 hours
five days a week and walked 2-3 hours a day and
memorised the suff I had learned, so no, I do not
miss it. There are fine memories like the morning
training privately with the teacher in in the garden
of the castle. The evenings were tuff, 1.5 hour

training, change of T-short, another 1.5 hours and then one more for the road.

The best thing was that I had arranged it so that I did not have to worry about bills and other boring things during that time. I did not see much of Ireland but I was wiser next time, hired a car when I had my days off and learned to know the country by driving to different places. I sold my car and hired my flat to a stranger to be able to stay away so long time. It was my choice and also a dream. Now I do not want to do it, no longer. The longest tome I have only trained was nine months but the hours spent every day was not so huge like in Ireland but I guarantee, it started to be quite heavy in the end of the day.

The nice thing with living months in one place is that you learn to know a bit more of the culture, habits and traditions in the country. You are not going to learn everything but you learn quite a few things and even some people. Martial arts society is like a big family, you always find some family members you like and can trust in. Even during a shorter visit you can learn a lot by talking with the local martial artists. Nowadays I prefer talk about everything but MA, when having a dinner together or some other social activity. My hobby and passion had taken me to places I never had visited voluntarily, but I am happy I did it.

Travelling at work

I have often met tired professional at airports who work very intensively in foreign countries, visit their family and hit the road again after a short break. I doubt that they would describe their travelling in work as pleasant and as a cultural exchange but surely exciting and rewarding in many ways. I interviewed once engineers and IT-specialists who travel six months every year controlling the condition of the railway with advanced equipment. They live in hotels and spend the days, long hours, on the rail.

They sit in a speciellt build carriage and tell the same jokes, which become well known after six months. One of the engineers told me that his wife would like to travel cross the country by rail, and live in fine hotels. The travelling is free for him and his family and hotels almost free. He told me that he cannot do that. I have also interviewed an individual who flies almost every day in work and travel with his wife almost every week-end and every vacation. He told that they are different things. He loves to be with his wife, where, does not matter for him.

Then there are the lucky ones like my ex who can stay at the conference city some extra days on holiday. I have been lucky too, I could teach all over the Europé, my passion, tai chi and the conditions are quite human. I did not work so much, in big international meetings, maybe only two, three hours a day. It was very satisfying both professionally and from private point of view. I teached and teach people, who really wanted/wants. In the evenngs you can enjoy interesting discussions with the local people discussions in the evening.An average tourist seldom get the same chances for discussions. I took the flight normally on thursday, had my books and newspapers with me and was often still reading when the plane landed. Most often, there were not so many passangers, so everything was easy and fast and I could spread my thing over three seats. I was less stressed at airports compared when I travelled private. I reasoned like this, if I am in right place in right time I have done my part. If there are delays it is not my fault and I can be cool. When travelling private, every delayed hour is my vacation, that becomes shorter, so it is of utmost importance that everything functions perfectly, well it is not always the case.

I had often the provilegium to choose the hotel. I prefered guesthouses instead of huge concrete and glass monsters, where the personal smile and say, thank you sir, yes sir. I was in the alps, in a motell, where the owners played cards with their friends, smoked and drank wine. When I finished my work and went to the motel to pick up my key and have a beer, the owner reluctantly left the table and served me, with the disappointed and defiant expression on his face. I thought that it is better than cold professionalism, it was authentic and I knew I could use it later, in a short story or tell it when eating dinner with friends.

I could not afford to stay extra days on my work trips. I had though more free time than the most who travel in work.

For example Björn Borg after finishing his career as a tennis player, started to visit the same places where he had competed. He had only seen the hotel room and tennishall.

I also think it is interesting that, in our time with technological equipment, that allows us to have meetings via internet, people travel more than before. It is still important to meet people. Maybe traveling can function also some kind of bonus, reward that more qualified jobs have.

Working on trips, boost your creativity.

For a writer, working while travelling and in different countries is possible and it is often more easy to focus on the work without all the distractions at home. The demands of everyday life are not present. When you are sitting in a bus or aeroplane, you cannot go and make a sandwhich or start to cleaning your home, if you are really desperate.

My best ideas I have got in trains, on flights, basicly when moving somewhere. I do not need to write, I am only planning in my mind, sometimes I write but if you have thought and planned everything, the actual writing goes fast.

I was a projectleader during three years acouple of years ago, and our speciality was to share our knowledge about people who had difficulties with attention. We should write a book about the whole project and naturally what were the results. I was sitting and writing in a train and came to this idea, that just the activity I was doing would be impossible to a person with concentration difficulties. If you are writing in a train you have to be able to concentrate on writing, but at the same time remember to check that you do not miss your station. You have to be aware of this. You have to ignore kids who are shouting and fighting and the parents who does not seem to care abou it. The middle age man, who is drunk and would love to talk with anybody but is actually annoying everybody, is a challenge. You have to watch your luckage and money and telephone. You have to stifle the impulses to move around or to go to have a coffee. Quite many of us can cope with this but if you have a chemical unbalance in your brain, already one of the mentioned interferences is enough to make it impossible to concentrate. I used this as an example, how to try to communicate to the big audience, what it meas to have concentration problems.

I was waiting for a train early in the morning when a long distance train came to the station. All the people seemed to look down, as they did, writing something, planning a meeting or the days program, maybe reading. It looked a little bit funny, it looked like dance performance with a choreography. A well known phenomen is that when we become too stressed, we all get problems with attention. I have experienced it too, running around like a mad man but not getting anything done.

Artists and writers have always tried to travel away in order to be able to concentrate better somewhere else. All these residencies are there for a reason. I got once the possibility to get money and write where I wanted. I took a last minute flight to Mallorca I thought I had booked a hotel in the city but found myself in a tourist hell with only hotels everywhere. I did not write anything there and I did not have good time. I was happy to go back home.

One of my teachers in creative writing has made an artform of applying sholarship. She is more than seventy but always on her way to write in Athens or only 100 km away on the countryside, in a residency. Her income is very low, so she uses her brain and writing to get a lifestyle she wants to have.

Be tourist in your own neighbourhood

It is quite natural state of mind to be curious and interested of the place you visit first time. You have to be, if you do not stay indoors all the time and use taxi for tranportatation, if needed. Everything we see and hear is different what we are used to. If our curiosity is not present and we lack that motivation to explore, so most of us want to manage and utilize our environment. It is a strong motivation and makes us to search a lot of information.

What if we would be as interested in our hometown or place we live in? When I was photographing in Punavuori in Helsinki and Barcelona, it was thrilling to think about how it looked only fifty years ago. Both places had a high criminality compared to the rest of the city at that time. Now both places had people with highest income in the city and the most creative, often artistic kind of work. Punavuori was the most violent place in the whole town and nowadays you could not find a more safe place. Galleries, sushibars, young welldressed people, people jogging in the streets etc.

Have you seen the museums of your own city? Galleries? How about the history of the place if you live on the countryside? Try citywalks in your hometown. I promise you, that it will be a surprise, a pleasant one. Every place on earth has something interesting to tell.

Especially big cities have endless possibilities to do things and participate and many things are free. I once went to a free theater rehearsal. I had seen the half of the play when I finally understood that it was the wrong theater and play. It was also free and so I had the original left to go to.

There is a famous song, where the text claims that nothing ever happens. The song have several layers, if you listen carefully. In high school we were complaining that nothing happened. I think it was more the age and we wanted to have action and adventures.

I worked in a harbour when I was studying. One old stevedore told us stories about old times, when women did all the heavy lifting and carrying. He sended us to voyages to different times and it was exciting and we also learned something University cannot teach you.

Reluctance to be a tourist

There was an interesting articel in a newspaper about travelling (Anna-Stina Nykänen HS 21.1.2016). It was about our reluctance to be tourists. It is best to let her speak.

" Many of my coworkers are always on the run: On vacation, travelling because of studies or because of work. Not a s tourists, it is an ugly word. They are helping in Tanzania, to get more cultural in Milan, to meet relatives in Paris or they only retreat to Thailand to write a book or some paper they need for their examen. After they come back they sigh that they should need to go somewhere. A journey to Berlin or Copenhagen are no longer cnsidered as travelling".

I think that it is interesting that Berliners themselves have started to consider foreigners living in Berlin as a problem. They have forgotten that big part of the dynamic of the city is created by all these talented, creative sometimes rich foreigners. The locals think that the prices of food and flats are going up, because of the foreigners and this is also partly true. Everybody can not live in Nice, London or Berlin, many of us want and the prices go up. I do not think Berliners would like their city more, if it was considered the last place on earth, people want to visit.

The world traveller Ernest Hemingway liked to give the impression that he knew everybody, even the personal and the owners of hotels and restaurants and also local people. They were often described as friends, not only professionals. The truth is that he was one of the team protected by Gertrude Stein and they all were quite separated from the local people, even french people in general, they formed their own subsociety or community.

In fiction the writer has the freedom and right to write what he/she wants. There are writers that go and count the stairs of a building to give the accurate number. I think it serves and satisfies more the author than the reader. The work does not become more or less authentic if the number of the stairs of the University is right or not.

Anyway one thing is sure, not only writers tell lies and exaggerate how much they have travelled. American saying sums up the matter: Been there, seen it, done that. We all boast sometimes about our travelling and other things. Sometimes the problem is that if travelling is your lifestyle you talk about it and others can interprete it in a negative way. My experience is that the longer time you have been for example living in another country, the less you talk about it, it is part of you. When making shorter jouneys our senses ar open for new influences, nuances and differences. If you stay a long time it becomes the normal state of affairs and there is no point talking about it, is there?

Travelling can also calm us down and make us behave in a more human and caring way. One professional in tourism told me how the stressed businessmen from Helsinki came to north of Sweden and Norway on vacation with their families for skiing. The first days they are busy talking with clients in the mobile phone, demanding better service, complaining about many things. The third day the personal got better contact with the businessmen and they started to be more relaxed, telling jokes, smoking and relaxing. The hotel actually listened to their critics and could improve their service from year to year. A lot of this travelling stopped when the ferries could no longer sell tax free products because of EU regulations. Maybe the italian man has right, in this case without cheap alcohol, a big number of people stopped completely to travel to this remote place.

When I was teaching tai chi in the monastery of Valamo I was told about the conference for psychoanalysts. The norwegian group was asking where the night club was, well no nightclubs in a monastery. When the same group left the monastery after the conference, they were pleased, relaxed and happy. There was a good sauna near the lake and they were served beer, sausage and of course good lunch and dinner. It was enough for these experienced travellers, who knew what they wanted and took it. Now they were happy with beautiful nature and sauna and swimming and maybe they had more interesting discussions with the colleges sitting around a fireplace instead of in a noisy nightclub.

Travelling in your work 2; experiences from a campsite

It is not always a must to travel yourself to experience things. I was responsible for the most beautiful campsite I know, in Pyhäjoki Finland. Yes it is the Pyhäjoki where they are prepairing and building for a nuclear plant and the builder is Rosatom, the russian company tightly connected to Putin and producing even nuclear weapons. The question if this was a wise thing to do, had divided people in different groups. There were activists from Germany, Sweden, Finland etc. The guestion was not only about moral and ethics and the protection of the future generations. It was a guestion of compensation and how much and when. Some property owners could not accept, that somebody could force them to sell and move away.

Put in a more dramatic way, I was a traveller in modern industrial history among other things, also a guestion of civil disobedience and power became very important. I could follow this because the activists sometimes hired our cottages,.The specialists who made their measurement came and went away very fast, they cost money and last but not least the leader of the community and the Rosatom representants and local companies had meetings and dinners, lunches at our place. At the same time the builders of wind power were the biggest group of clients. The world came to me. Everybody was telling me their opinion and why they thinked in this or that way. The tourists were also fun to meet. They were in good mood, in no hurry and they told me everything from how the weather had been when they left Norway or Germany, to more private things like relationproblems etc. I even learned to know all the good and bad roads with construction zones. I liked to talk with the customers, locals aswell as those who came from Latin America and Indien.

I as not suffering of remote belonging, the world literally came to me, the hunger of world did not go away. I was also working 24/7, the most nights I could sleep but we accepted guests 24 hours, instead of closing latest 21.00 like even the big campsites did and still do.

The beautiful place by the river helped to have the power to work constantly. The first summer I teached tai chi and had cattle bell training every morning for our guests and local people, I have very nice memories of that time with sunny, fantastic mornings, training outside and having fun with the customers. Several icecream byers told us that they had been workin in the campsite as teenagers and remembered it as the best summer they had had in their lives.

The last comments about living abroad and to be immigrant

To study or work abroad has become more common thanks to EU and all the efforts made to make exchange of students and working in different countries possible. I think it is very important. Livin abroad becomes naturally normal very fast. There are some things that are harder to adapt, like the fact that in Switcherland women normally stay at home with kids and serve lunch everyday, when the children come home to eat at luchtime. Otherwise we start to onsider everything as normal

Some part of the readjustment is harmless and easy. You learn fast to have cappuccino in the morning, never after dinner. I had a finnish friend with me in Italy and after a seminar we had a dinner party in the evening. I told my friend that it would be better take espresso after dinner but he insisted to have cappuccino.I think it is OK but he got tired answering 23 people, why he was having cappuccino. You adapt fast after these occasions. In Italy there is one really good rule, and it is that it is not considered good behaviour to be drunk in social context.

In Nice all the things we normally want to have when buying a flat are no nos there. A balcony giving towards south is a good idea in the north, in the south you should avoid it, it simply gets too hot to be there in summer time and the whola flat gets heated. We prefer to be able to walk or cycle to the restaurant but forget about it. In south you take the car. I do not like Nice in the summer time, it is too hot, too many tourists and the light is much more clear and beautiful in the winter time. When you watch to the sea from the mountains in summer you only see fog everywhere. In the winter you see everything in a fantastic clear light, this is the reason so many painters have been living there. A little similar light exist on Skagen, Denmark, where also many famous painters have worked.

Nice is compared to a woman who has an evening dress but has wellies on. I have never experienced glamour in Nice and I have lived there for years. I visited once hotel Negresco, due to a lecture I wanted to listen. That was maybe the nearest I came to experience glamour. I used to take long walks along the coast line in Cap Ferra, where you could see walls of the rich peoples houses. Normally the only person present was the gardener, Elton John, Beckham etc are busy men.

I got he opportunity to teach languages at a company Monaco, when I lived in Nice for the first time. Monaco had good salaries but I do not like the atmosphere, only rich people and surveillance cameras, maybe it is only the money I envy? As a curiosity I can mention, that I was served very good coffee at the company in Monaco. I asked how come the coffee could be so good, at that time coffee machines in companies were quite bad, or frankly, the coffee was terrible.

The high quality of coffee was thanks to the highest boss in Europe, who loved coffee, a finnish man. Finland is leading coffee consumer in the world but the coffee is actually quite not very good. One friend of mine refused to drink finnish coffee after working in Italy some time. I understand him.

Unfortunately I moved fom Nice so I only had time to teach swedish, later on I should even have teached finnish but it did not happen. T thought it was somewhat comical to teach these small languages in Monaco!

I have often had fun about the attitude, mediterrian people have concerning winter. When the calender says it is winter, then it is. It means that offices etc do not use air con, although it is more than +30. Women change to winter boots, especially in Spain this was/is important. I understand the importance of change.

It is strange how fast we adjust to a new upset of rules, customs and habbits. We start to consider the new land's norms as standard and do not question them anymore. This helps us to live our normal life and spares our energy. An interesting thing can happen, we can start to evaluate our home country norms and values with a little more opened mind than before.

People who have lived a long time in China tell the same story. After coming back to Scandinavia they wondered, were are all the people hiding? Big empty plazas and places totally empty. It can create angst. A swedish businessman told that he found his japanese guests under the table in the hotellroom. The japanese could not understand that a city with more than a million inhabitants can be empty on a sunday morning. They had looked out and were convinced that the big one was coming. Alternative was some other catastrophe like nuclear disaster, and they had been instructed to seek cover in the case of earthquake.

Even you live in another country only a limited time, so part of the experience is, how does it feel to be immigrant. It doesnot mean anything, that you are not one. You are going to be treated as one. Liisa Helve-Sibaja has described this in her book. When you read this, please remember that the family is well off, even measured by swiss standards. I hope Liisa accepts my somewhat free translation: The officiel image of immigrants is at it's best questionable. I do not want to belong that minority, but I do. We immigrants have hard to adapt properlyto the rules in the society. We rob jewelry shops, aswell as private houses. We cause trafic jams, because we are too stupid to learn the system of alternate advance right, called the zipper system. We fill the trains, buy houses for miljons and cause a haute in the market. We even take the jobs from swiss people, we conquer the country and demand all kinds of things. Source, Hausfrau, at home in Switcherland.

The welfare state of Sweden was created with the heavy export industry products, the source is Swedish University and officiel statistics. In this, often dangerous and dirty work were in the sixties as many as 8 foreigners of ten, to make it simple. Six of these eight were finnish people, so it is not out of the blue that finnish people was a strong factor, when creating the wealth needed to build wellfare state, never seen before. Unfortunately, it is not going to be repeted anymore. So why immigrants are always targeted as problems? Finnish people were working so hard that they ruined the system, that was build as an alternative to get paid per hour. Many authors wittness the need to work double so hard as swedish people, to be accepted.

Nowadaysit is totally accepted to be so called critical against immigrants. Last time I visited Finland after having spent two years in different countries. This is what I met at the airport. My cappuccino was served by an Asian, the cafe floor was cleaned by a black woman and the flight bus was droven by an indian person. I had to fix my tooth, that had been damaged and the dentist was from Baltic countries. How could we manage without these people?

I have had a photo exhibition round the country, about my tour through Europe. It is nothing compared to when people are forced to leave their homes, because of war or starving, often both.

It is also so, that we cannot stop living our lives or feel bad that we can afford enjoy our lives.

Hopefully travelling makes us more tolerant and solidaric. More on this topic in the next chapter.

Change of perspective- do traveling open and broaden our minds?

There is a cliche that traveling broadens your mind. It can and it does but in the worst case scenarios, we connect our stereotypes with new ones. I have seen many collegues and students to pick up from his/her martial art things that suits them and connecting them to other things they already liked before. It is totally acceptable for everyone to build their own system they believe in. It is another boll game if they start to sell their personal believes as Universal truths and make money on them.

Stereotypes are not only untrue but they also limit the possibility to create something new. We try to make things and the world more simple, stereotypes are useful in this project, but it is not the correct pic.

As a child I was afraid of Pippi Longstocking. I considered her as an impossible figure. She is all that, still now through an adult's eyes. The only thing has changed that imbarassed fear, has transformed to admire. She has th cuts to see the things from a different perspective, or if you want, she is different and thinks differently. She has traveled with his father and she does not respect or believe the local authorities, lärarn, socialworkers, not even police. She is joking and making fun of these grounpelars of the society.

She creates her own rule. She goes to school only to get holidays. She is physically stronger than adults.

I was terrified about the fact, that she was living alone. Her mother was dead and father, perhaps alive, sailing the sevev seas as a

pirate. Now I understan why she made me afraid and why I did not even like her as a child. She is still frightening me, I suppose.

She is not only creating own rules but breaking every norm there is. She buys too much candies, destroys kafferep. As an adult you could describe her as a creative person, who has the ability to change perspective. She is economically independent. She has a natural, good relation to her dead mother

The only thing that is sure is that Pippi or me had stayed in our small communities utan travelling, we had accepted the values and norms of the society as our own. Pippi can sees as a representant of one of the extreme ends of a continuum, considering what travelling do with people. She became very tolerant, indeed. The other end could be the swedish gentleman, who only found faults and bad things in the country he visited. Most of us are more in the middle of th Gaus curve.

In an interesting documentary, young finnish professionals were intervjued, after many years studies in different countries. One young professional told that even the teachers came from different countries. It was impossible not to learn one thing. Everything can be done in thousand different ways. It helped him to find his own expression and to be critical

Esa-Pekka Salonen, nowadays dirigent in London Symphonie orchestra, has told how USA, Los Angeles really made him more free and find his own way. He did not feel the pressure of European culture and heritage.

I found out, when teaching in Germany, France and Switcherland that the famous teachers who had been writing books, were normal human beings, with their own faults, both professional level and private level. I think little countries, like Scandinavien countries do have too much respect to bigger countries. Interesting thing about USA, at least in my profession is that the spectrum is so much wider. The highest level and lowest level is far beyond, at least Scandinavien countries.

The positive thing in USA is that you can say you are good. In Scandinavien there is a strange mentality, that says you should be humble. My teacher who used to come to Sweden and Finland to teach always told me that our humbledness was lying. You should tell the truth and why to take cover behind an attitude you are no good, even the opposite is lying, to exaggerate your skilllevel.

I learned my lession long time ago. Respect everybody from different countries and listen and learn but do not think they are better, only because they are good in talking. I am quite good in talking too but my dream is that we could have authentic meetings between professionals. It is a good goal, I think.

Sustainability

I believe that the swedish schoolgirl Greta Thunberg has right. Her point is that politicans, parents, yes indeed all adults are, if not lying so not doing anything. Maybe words but no action. I am one of them and it is the first time in history, that the older generation leaves behind a world that is in worse state compared when they inherited it. Probably there is soon nothing we can call legacy.

Greta started to demonstrate against climate change in Stockholm every friday and now it is a global movement that I hope will make a difference. At least they try and we should be ashamed.

so how come I advocate travelling with my opinions? Well, I believe there are a lot of things to do without a total stop for travelling.

There is of course the political level, where the most important decisions has to be made but we can as citizens do quite a lot already.

Greta got his parents to become vegeterians and start using train in their travels, allthough her mother is a famous operasinger.

We can all make this choice. At the same time there is interesting research going on to get clean fuel to aeroplanes, which takes away 80 % of the damaging carbon dioxide.

We can choose to explore our own country instead of longtravel and use bicycle as a way to transport in cities we visit. To bicycle from one wineyard to another is not a bad way to use one's vacation. Already slow travelling and human modernists were discussed and both are also good for a more sustainable travelling.

I believe that politicans have to make the important decisions and we should influence them, to make sometimes hard decicions and help them to achieve the goals. There is no time left, maybe it is too late already but we have to make a try and hope technology will do the rest, if not today so maybe tomorrow.

If it was possible to transport heavy ironstone with electric train to harbour, where sailing ships took the cargo to foreign countries more than 100 years ago, so we really can do everything that is needed to do, today.

I do take a flight quite often, eventhough I could have chosen the train. Actually this is due to the pricesetting. If I have to travel between two countries when working and the train cost ten times more and takes 20 times more time, so I am not saying sorry.

When I was working in Zurich last year, I used biycle in and even out of the city to 98 %. It was simply the fastest solution in the city. I did not want to experience the nature sitting in a metallbox, so bicycle was the best way. It also kept me fit. In London, same year, the fastest way to move was Underground. Those few times I had to pick up things with a car, it took five times more time compared to train. In Scotland I lived in so little city that even bicycle was unnecessary, locals did drive everywhere but it is another story. In Portugal and France bicycle was faster than buses/train etc. Toscana is one of the places like Lappland and of course many other places, where car can be the best way to explore the countryside, especially if your time is limited.

Carbon dioxide is not the only problem with travelling, as described in this book what concerns for example AirBnB.

The focus in this book was not the problems but overall things connected to travelling. Travelling can be and is a positive thing. Not only as a recreation but to broaden people's views and hopefully making them more tolerant against other people and cultures.

After a book review, I bought a book I was convinced I would dislike. The opposite happened. Why I bought the book in the first place because of one sentence I got interested, " The hunger of world increases by travelling, the hunger of life by dreaming" (from the book, White couche on Riviera, author Merja Tynkkynen). I like words and sentences and thaughts. One thought in one day is actually enough. For a writer one good sentence is enough. I thought this book was one of the many, written by people who are enough well off, to afford living in French Riviera and who have had or are having a profession, which makes them consider themselves capable to write books.

Being expert, for example in economics, does not necessarily make you an author. Merja is already in the business and the book was entertaining. She is really being honest about, why she wanted a house, in a place too many wants to live. After quite much struggling, she finds out, that her Mediterrian idealisation and need to fly away from the everyday life is the desire to have a fresh start. She compares it with, when a fifty years old man want to have a divorce and marries a younger woman.

The possibility to have a fresh beginning, scandinaviens call it "clean or empty table", tabula rasa, interests many but maybe it is a dream?

Marco Polo's travels

Marco Polo's journeys are like The Canterbury tales located in the middle age. Marco Polo had no education but could tell about foreign countries, deras geography, architecture, commerce, armies, warfare etc. He did this without using religious concepts. Actually people did not believe his stories, at leasr the contempary people. The numbers, amounts of things seemed to an ordinary european as fantasy figures. He was called miljon Marco, eventually. One thing is sure that sometimes he was carried away and did tell invented stories, although he had a sharp intellect. There is another possibility to this, why he seemed to tell lies sometimes. The stories were written by a convict in prison and there is no quaranties, that the authors knowledge in language used, was the best possible.

Traveling seemed to be much more interesting long time ago. It was and it was far more dangerous than nowadays. The reason why pilgrime routes were long way from coastal regions, was that coasts were not safe. The pilgrims carried a long stick with sharp metal tip. It was for selfdefence against bandits and wild animals. Traffic is the biggest danger nowadays, also dogs are a problem.

We can also check many places on google maps. It was far more exciting to hear stories from the seas, told by some boys who left the school and became sailors. You used your imagination to fill the gaps and it was so exciting! I maybe have a romantic view on this topic. The reality on sailing boats was everything else but romantic life. There was one advantage before, and it was also partly due to it, the romantic image appeared. The boats stayed in the harbours long enough, to explore and get a glimt of other cultures, maybe even beyond the bars of the port or nearest city. Roll off- roll on makes the necessary stops as short as possible and the crew is slimmed so that a very little group of people keeps the boat moving all the time.

we come back to Marco Polo a little while. It is not easy to judge what is true and what isn't, when you read his books. He tells about a Tibetan custom, where mothers offer their daughters to rich merchants and the merchants give girls jewels. When the girls will marry, the girl who has most jewels, is the most wanted. After marriage, this behavior is no longer accepted. He also write about people, who are bad and do not consider robbery or theft as bad? It could be true. Moral is always connected to the cultur and historic time. It is not a long time ago, you were allowed to kill people without address. The legislation still gives the police right to fine peoplewithout address in UK.This law camea after Napoleon wars, when men came back and wanted to havea job, but they were too many. In Sweden they wrongly talk about finnish gypsies. They all have swedish names but a new said that male gypsy can be killed on the street without any legal action what so ever. Well, they fled to Finland. Otherwise they had been stupid, more accurately, dead.

Anyway I think it was more exciting to tell about adventures in faraway countries.

Visions of the future travelling

It is interesting to seewhat happens with travelling in the near future. Different tendencies are influencing. On one side technological achievements and on the other side the demand of sustainability.

Supersonic flights are banned for the moment but whatif we get new fuel or new engines or power generators of some kind. Hyperloop is already a serious alternative and there is promise that cargo and people will be transported in three, four yearsfrom now on. WIG (Wing In Ground Effect) are already used. I am convinced, that new inventionswill come, it is time for that and the demands to try to save our planet should speed up the process. We are capable of both saving the planet and travel, even travel fast, if necessary.

When military needed better equipment for communication and orientation, it was simply fixed very fast and the world got web and mobile phone as a consequence of this decision and the development that was generated by that decision. It would be a peace of cake to solve our problems if we really try our best. It will also boost our economics. The mantra that we cannot afford to change the world is faulse. It is a fact that we cannot afford not to change it. We just has to make a decision like that we did, when we send a man to moon, with ridiciously little knowledge. Yes Kennedy did it but we can do it again. World wide web and smartphones needed also decisions. Cannot we make one decent decision. We have to. How can we otherwise leave this world to our children and grandchildren?

Coming home

To come home and settle down takes some time. There was a time, when I came home, I thaught I will stay a year before next time. After sleeping one night properly, I was ready to new adventures. So is not the case anymore. I can be on the road even longer time than before, I am more free from responsibilities, but when I land it seems to take more time to adapt. Maybe it is agood thing? It is sometimes good to check and value how things have been, maybe in the big picture aswell, life in general. Even if life is happening, when we make other plans, freely according John Lennon so from time to time it is good to check the situation. It is like checking rear view mirror. The faster the car or life goes, the more important is it to check the past.

One way to keep yourself up to date of your own situation is to write down your travelexperiences. Some kind of diary is also useful if you write professionally or want to remember names of places, people, interesting things etc.

I have tried to avoid write about the normal things when trekking, sore muscles, aching feet or back etc. I also did not photograph at all for many, many years on my travels. I did not want to put something between my eyes and the reality. Also I noticed that I was not enjoying the nature but thinking about good or interesting camera angle, light etc. The most extreme situation is for the pressphotographer who is taking photos of people who are dying, instead of helping them. This being said, they do very important work and the latest years, way too many have lost their lives, doing their important work. I only try to explain my attitude. I have just come home after being away one year in four different countries, without taking photos. I assure I remember everything, staying minimum three months in one place. When writing about traveling, I do take photos and will make notes.

Even before I was waiting homecoming impariently if I had been learning my martial arts in Asien or elsewhere. I loved to come home and study and start to learn properly the material I had with me. Learning abroad is often a bit stressfull but to slowly make the new stuff your own at home was to me the best part of everything. I have the same attitude to all of my travels nowadays. All the material, memories, experiences, scents, colours, voices, noise are good to unload slowly, withou stress. The longer you have been away, the longer it takes before I start to check pics, analyze what happened and eventually write about it. I fully trust the process that happen without being aware of it. If you try too much, it will only stop or interfere with the process. The best way is to let go and let the things happen, when they happen.